THE VW BEETLE

A Production History of the World's Most Famous Car
1936–1967

Ryan Lee Price

HPBOOKS

HPBooks
are published by
The Berkley Publishing Group
A division of Penguin Group (USA)
375 Hudson Street
New York, New York 10014

First edition: September 2003
ISBN: 1-55788-421-8

10 9 8 7 6 5 4 3 2 1

This book has been catalogued with the Library of Congress

Book design and production by Michael Lutfy
Cover photo courtesy Volkswagen AG
Cover design by Bird Studios
Interior photos and illustrations by the author unless otherwise noted

ACKNOWLEDGMENTS

This book could not have been possible without the support and encouragement of my wife Kara, the patience of my editor, Michael Lutfy, and the photographic assistance of Volkswagen of America, Volkswagen de Mexico, Volkswagen AG, *VW Trends* magazine, and the photography collections of Terry Shuler, James Brooks and Carsten Reeder.

ABOUT THE AUTHOR

Ryan Lee Price is currently the editor of *VW Trends* magazine, an internationally circulated Volkswagen magazine that caters to the aircooled VW enthusiasts of the world. He and his wife Kara, an elementary school teacher, live in Corona, California. Aside from many published fiction stories and articles in a variety of fields and periodicals, this is Price's first book.

It is difficult to say who should receive credit for the Volkswagen Beetle, but there is no doubt that two people had more to do with its creation than any other—Adolph Hitler and Ferdinand Porsche. Porsche had the dream of emulating Henry Ford by providing "every man" with an affordable car, while Hitler saw it as an opportunity to empower his citizens and, in the process, bolstering his own hold over his countrymen during his rise to power. The Beetle was developed in the shadows of one of the darkest periods in human history, yet it emerged virtually unscathed, embarking on a path to becoming the "world's most popular car." Although there were some who upheld the VW Beetle as a symbol of Nazism, most fell in love with the cute little Bug.

So it is hard to imagine the world without the Volkswagen Beetle. More than 21 million have been built, and you can still see millions of them on city streets, mountain roads, in driveways and buzzing down freeways in almost every corner of the world.

Beetles have been owned by a variety of devoted owners. Many name their "Bugs"—Ladybug, June Bug, Pumpkin, and of course, the Love Bug (how many companies can say their car has starred in several movies?). They are easy to work on (if/when they break down), simple to operate, and economical to own. They're talked to, cared for, restored to impeccable condition or customized to outrageous proportions. They evoke smiles and hand waving from one owner to another, and they have what would seem like a cult following that crosses many modern socio-economic boundaries.

The Beetle was resurrected in United States in the late 1990s, after having been absent since 1979, beginning yet another chapter in this story that may never end.

How to Use This Book

The first portion of this book is a chronological history of the Beetle, the major designers, engineers and businessmen responsible for its development during the years from 1936 through 1967. In the second section, "Volkswagen by the Numbers," the factory changes are categorized in calendar years, not model years. For example, the changes made to the 1966 Beetle are listed in the chapters covering calendar years 1965 and 1966, because production of the 1966 Beetle began on August 1, 1965 and ended July 31, 1966.

Conversely, for example, in the chapter covering the calendar year 1966, both the changes for the 1965 and 1966 Beetles are represented because they were both produced in that calendar year. At the beginning of each chapter, the chassis and engine numbers for both the calendar year (Jan. 1 through Dec. 31) and the model year (Aug. 1 through July 31) are listed when available.

The production changes in each chapter are listed chronologically, as they were made at the factory, not alphabetically or in subsections as done in other books. At the beginning of each change listed, a category is introduced (chassis, electrical, etc.). Not only does this give the reader a better feel for the random changes that were made on the factory floor, the parts suppliers and through the design process, but he can quickly scan through the year to locate a specific period of time. Despite its never-changing shape, the Volkswagen Beetle was under constant revision throughout its production run and has been one of the most enduring designs in automotive history. *Ryan Lee Price*

PART I:
A
PRODUCTION
HISTORY
OF THE
"PEOPLE'S CAR"

PORSCHE AND THE EARLY VOLKSWAGENS

Reborn from the ashes of a destroyed country, a bombed-out factory and its thousands of refugee workers, the Volkswagen was forged by a handful of men who shared a vision that the world would soon realize. This vision of a car "for the people" didn't originate in a corporate environment, and the engineers didn't base their design on the research of test panels, focus groups and car-owner surveys. At that time, there were only dreams, pencils, paper and ideas. The money came later. The Beetle's characteristics, the combined building blocks that make it unique—the swing axle, central-tube frame, torsion bars, opposed aircooled engine at the rear and the beetle-like stream-lined shape—were the products of many men and generated from almost 40 years of designs, tests and implementations.

Ferdinand Porsche

Although the Beetle was ultimately the final product developed by a score of designers and engineers, most historians will agree that Ferdinand Porsche is the man who brought the Beetle from concept to completion. Porsche had always dreamed of a car in concept to Henry Ford's Model T, a car affordable and available to every man, not just the elite.

Before the Beetle, Porsche had already designed small cars for several manufacturers, but many never made it past the prototype stage into mass production, and those that did were much too expensive for the average citizen. Unlike America, most of the European carmakers were stubbornly clinging to the expensive handcrafted cars that only a few could afford, rather than risk venturing into the mass-produced market. Why

An automotive genius, Ferdinand Porsche dreamed of a car for the common man, inspired by Henry Ford's Model T. He persevered after many years, overcoming stiff opposition from many European competitors.

This is the headquarters for Porsche's design studio in Stuttgart, Germany, which he established in 1930. The parking lot was usually filled with many prototypes and various designs.

impressive to note that he didn't have any formal training with electricity, only the ingenuity and talent for engineering. Upon seeing what his son had accomplished and his zest for the burgeoning technology, Anton Porsche couldn't help but be impressed. As a result, and after much persuading from his mother, Ferdinand was sent off to study at a trade school in Riechenberg. There he took classes in the Werkmeisterschule to learn to be a factory foreman. But he was also able to expand his knowledge of electricity and engineering.

After graduation, Porsche left for Vienna, at the time known as one of the technological centers in Europe, and attended the Technical University of Vienna. He did so improbably, given that he had the lowest grades in his class the year before at the Werkmeisterschule. Soon thereafter, he landed his first job with the firm United Electrical Company, owned by Bela Egger (later to be known as the Brown Boveri organization). His first duties were sweeping the shop floors and greasing machinery, but it wasn't long before his inquisitive mind landed him a position in the experimental shop. In 1898, Porsche was promoted to manager of the test department and first assistant in the calculating section. It was during this time when he met and fell in love with another United Electrical employee, Aloisia Kaes, whom he married on October 17, 1903.

In 1898, at the age of 23, he acquired a job in the shop of Jacob Lohner, owner of a long-established carriage factory in Vienna, who had been building electric cars and was impressed by Porsche's designs. Porsche set to work improving the Lohner plans, and two years later, built a battery-powered car of his own that was shown at the 1900 Paris Exhibition. He won the grand prize for his car. One year after this, he designed, built and tested an electric-gas powered hybrid called the Lohner-Porsche Mixt. It did away with batteries, and instead used a gasoline-

abandon a lucrative market when there were still rich people willing to purchase ornate automobiles? But Porsche refused to give up on his dream.

He was born in Maffersdorf, Austria, on September 3, 1875, the son of a conservative tinsmith named Anton, who didn't subscribe to his son's belief in the future of engineering, electricity and automobiles. It was a given that young Ferdinand would follow in his father's footsteps and enter into the family business, and as the eldest son, someday take it over. But Ferdinand proved to be as stubborn as his father, and proceeded with his experiments with electricity in the attic of his family's house, first without his father's knowledge (with his mother's support) and then to his father's disapproval. At the age of 15, his life was changed when he went on a call to fix a drain at the carpet shop of Willy Ginskey. There, Ginskey had rigged an electric light bulb in his shop, and it was just the inspiration Porsche needed. Two years later, in 1892, Porsche wired the house with electricity, adding incandescent lights, electric chimes and even an intercom. All of this was done at an age when electricity was an extremely new medium, and it is powered engine to drive a generator that sent power to electrical motors attached directly to the front hubs. Lohner began to object to Porsche's expensive projects (of which he had no shortage of) and wanted to concentrate on selling the Mixt to the public. However, Porsche wasn't interested in marketing cars, only designing them, so in 1905, he moved to Austro-Daimler which had been interested in the designer for some time.

As Technical Director, he began to develop the ideas that would ultimately shape the Beetle. Daimler was building cars on a mass scale, but they still were very expensive. Porsche began his quest to develop a car for every man during this stage of his career, and there were several significant developments that would set him on this path.

In 1909, he designed a 32 hp passenger car with a four-speed gearbox, and three years later designed an aircooled aircraft engine that is regarded as the precursor to the first VW engine. In 1916, after winning several awards (Poetting Medal in 1905 and the Officers' Cross of Francis Joseph in 1916) he was given an honorary doctorate from the Technical University of Vienna.

However, Porsche continued to be frustrated by his employer. Austro-Daimler remained a luxury carmaker, and was making a fortune doing so. The company didn't want anything to do with mass production of inexpensive automobiles, and Porsche's dream for turning the luxury car producer into a mass-produced car manufacturer was met with much conflict.

His ideas for a small car increased tension in boardroom meetings and by 1923 he was out on the streets looking for another job. Because of the crippling post World War I economy, Porsche was hesitant in setting up his own business, so he embarked on a position as technical director with Daimler-Motoren-Gesellshaft based in Stuttgart, Germany. Though the two companies, Austro-Daimler and DMG are considered separate enterprises, they are both founded from the same families. It was here at this equally ostentatious car company that he designed the 7.1-liter SS and SSK of 1928, all the while pushing his ideas for a utilitarian vehicle for the masses. Again, his small-car ideas fell on equally deaf ears. His frustration came to a head when, after building 30 prototypes of a 1280cc, front-engine car, Daimler still decided not to put Porsche's car into production.

The following year, 1929, found Porsche again in Austria, this time working for Steyr. Before and during World War I, Steyr was known as J. & F. Wendl and Company, and was considered the largest gunsmith in the world, producing approximately three million rifles. When they branched out into making airplane engines for the first World War, producing cars was not far behind. Steyr enjoyed the advantage of having a large factory that could provide everything from the raw materials to the final product. Though his time at Steyr was short lived, Porsche did have time enough to design the Type Austria, his first design to use swing axles. However, the stock market crash in the U.S. took its toll on Europe as well, and Steyr was hit particularly hard. It was forced to merge with Porsche's old employer, Austro-Daimler, and became known as Steyr-Daimler-Puch.

Porsche had not left Austro-Daimler under the best of circumstances, so at the age of 54 he finally decided to become an independent designer. He soon opened a consulting office in Austria with his partner, Adolf Rosenberger (who owned 15 percent of the business and had a passion for auto racing), and his brother-in-law Dr. Anton Piëch.

At the end of 1930, Porsche moved to Stuttgart and had expanded to a staff of 12, one of whom was Karl Rabe, who had worked with Porsche and succeeded him at Austro-Daimler. The full name of the studio was, D. Ing h.c. F. Porsche GmbH, Konstruktionsbüro für Motoren, Fahrzeug

These are the Porsche headquarters in Stuttgart, where the KdF-Wagen as well as a variety of "people's cars" were designed and built. Although Porsche was never a supporter of the Nazi regime, it was the source of most all of his funding.

und Wasserfahrzeugbau, which roughly translates to mean that Porsche would also be interested in designing airplanes and amphibious planes to pay the bills. His offices were in what was called the Ulrich Building on Stuttgart's Kronenstrasse. His staff consisted of several close members of previous teams he had worked with at Daimler and Steyr. All of the men were Austrian, and most all lived at the shop. Karl Rabe, who had followed him from company to company throughout his career, was his chief designer and had the only room to himself. Other members of his staff were: Erwin Kommenda, who was in charge of car bodies (and later designed the shape of the post-WWII Porsche 356); Josef Zahradnik, who designed axles, suspension and steering; Karl Fröhlich, transmissions; and Josef Kales, who handled engine designs. Soon after the office opened, Reimspiess and Mickl joined the staff. Rosenberger was the business manager, something that Porsche admittedly wasn't good at. His main task was to curb the excited emotions of Porsche and his design team, and keep them within some sort of budget.

Karl Rabe

Although Porsche was the driving force behind his team, he was not the only man with design talents on his staff. Porsche had the ideas, but it was Karl Rabe who made them work. He began his career working with Porsche in 1913 at Austro-Daimler, and was present through the creative differences that Porsche experienced before leaving. Rabe stayed on until Porsche set up his own auto design consulting business in early 1931. Rabe couldn't resist the offer to work with Porsche as Chefkonstrukteur (Chief Designer). Some of Porsche's first contracts had been with Wanderer and Horch, two firms that would soon become part of Auto Union.

In August 1931, Porsche was granted the patent for an independent suspension system based on torsion bars instead of standard leaf springs. The money from royalties from the torsion bars was useful, and he immediately began work on what he called project number 12 (or Type 12), a small car for the everyman that was funded completely out of his own pocket, even though he didn't even have a client yet for the project. The con-

The early testing of prototype engines with two cylinders proved unreliable and down on power. Franz Reimpiess was given the task of coming up with an acceptable four-cylinder version and this is the result.

tracts from Wanderer and Horch allowed him some further financial freedom, but very little. Though his staff could have taken higher paying jobs at other manufacturers, they were very loyal to Porsche. Money was so tight that Porsche often borrowed on his life insurance or paid salaries in installments.

The Type 12 project was well timed, because, soon after, in September 1931, he met the president of Zündapp, Dr. Fritz Neumeyer. Zündapp was a successful motorcycle manufacturer in Nüremberg, but was struggling through a declining market and wanted something to help pull them out of it. Neumeyer, who was very receptive to the idea of a small car, initially came up with a concept car called the Klienauto. However, the actual production of such a car was beyond the expertise of his motorcycle engineers, so Neumeyer turned to Porsche and his design team. Porsche presented him with their Type 12, which Neumeyer agreed to build. Technically speaking, the Type 12 was very similar to the first Beetle.

The Type 12

During several meetings with the design teams of Zündapp, it was suggested that the Zündapp Volksauto (a popular name for any small "people's" car in 1920–30s Germany), or Type 12 as Porsche had been calling it, was to be a four-seat, two-door sedan with a swing-axle suspension and a one-liter (1000cc) engine. The car was intended to be structurally light and short, so it could achieve the targeted 35 mpg fuel consumption at an average speed of 40 mph. The chassis was a tubular design, supporting a single-sheet floor pan that was strengthened by several bent ridges throughout the pan and a tunnel that was formed along the centerline. Like the later Beetle, the rounded body would then be bolted to the pan to form a similar monocoque body like an airplane. Porsche insisted that Zündapp employ his independent torsion-style suspension that he had just invented as a means of calming the usual bumpy ride of a small car with both wheels sprung together, as the shock of the bump is then compounded by the entire axle's length. Porsche gave his designers 90 days to complete this task.

Initially, the Porsche team designed an air-cooled, four-cylinder boxer-type engine for the rear of the car. Surrounding it was a streamlined body made by Reutter coachworks in Stuttgartt, which was constructed of aluminum skins over a wooden frame (although the final production cars were to be made of all steel). When finished, it looked similar to what is now the Beetle. It was even rear-wheel driven.

The one-liter aircooled engines were built but the engineers at Zündapp insisted that a watercooled five-cylinder radial engine be used. They figured it would be quieter and more appealing to potential customers. Porsche conceded and for the presentation, produced three prototypes, as he always did. The new engines were built to the client's specifications at the Zündapp shop. They were 1200cc five-cylinder radial engines that produced roughly 26bhp. Mated with a three-speed transmission mounted in front of the engine with an overdrive gear, the Type 12 fail miserably on its initial tests. Since the radial engine was mounted in the rear, it received very little cooling air and rapidly overheated—only six miles down the road on the initial test drive. In addition to this, the five-cylinder engine was difficult to service, and the torsion bars failed easily, snapping all around the cars like rifle shots.

But these design failures were only part of the reason Zündapp decided not to produce the car. During the design process, and while the prototypes were being built, the company had a chance to analyze the costs of producing a small car and decided against it. In the end, they concluded that they would do best at sticking with motorcycles. None of the three little prototypes survive. While the fates of the first two are unknown (they were kept by Zündapp and probably scrapped), the third one was kept at Porsche's studio in Stuttgart and was destroyed in a bombing raid during the war.

Five varieties of KdF and/or Volkswagen logos were prepared for the new car's debut in Germany and to the world.

The Type 32

Learning from what he experienced with Zündapp, Porsche took more control with his future contracts, demanding additional creative and technical liberties. Although his plans for a small car were put on hold by the cancellation of the Zündapp project and there were no major contracts for his studio in 1932, he was approached the following year by NSU director Fritz von Falkenhayn and the idea was resurrected again.

NSU Works in Neckarsulm was another struggling motorcycle company, who had recently been forced to surrender their facility to the Italian carmaker, Fiat. But in 1933, the economy was springing back and NSU was ready to add a car to their inventory. Porsche had the designs almost ready before von Falkenhayn entered his office. The changes were mostly made to the body's shape. This time, the headlights were recessed into the front fenders and the body was much more streamlined.

Called the Type 32 by Porsche, the three prototypes produced for NSU were also rear-engine, this time with an aircooled flat-four 1470cc engine (at NSU's request), developing 26hp at the low engine speed of 2600rpm. There were several design elements that would soon become familiar. Porsche's new torsion bars were used on the front and rear wheels, with parallel trailing arms in front and swing axles in the rear. The three prototypes were completed in 1934, one made of all steel again by Ruetters, while the other two were clothed by a combination of wood floors and frame and a leather body, called the Weymann technique. The NSU cars were bigger and roomier than the Zündapp prototypes, and most important, they could be built cheaper.

Testing conducted in the Black Forest went off without any problems. After his first ride, von Falkenhayn was reported saying the loud engine, "sounds like a worn-out stone crusher." Nevertheless, he was impressed with the car's performance and its top speed of roughly 75 mph. Of course, Porsche still experienced problems with the snapping torsion bars, but while von Falkenhayn started preparations to get the car into production, Porsche streamlined his designs and worked on the initial flaws. Although Porsche's elation that his dream of the car for the "every man" was closer to production than ever, it was short-lived.

In the end, NSU, like Zündapp, was hesitant in entering the car market due to the surprisingly large amount of money it would take to get the Type 32 into production. Then, the deal was officially shattered when Fiat strongly reminded its German counterpart that they, according to their 1929 merger agreement, would refrain from building

In 1932, Porsche again stepped one foot closer to his goal of a car for every man with this prototype, the Type 32 for NSU. This had the flat-four engine in the rear as well as his patented torsion bars.

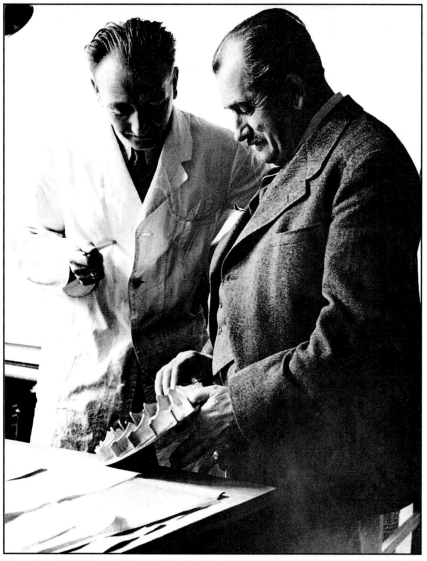

Porsche, at right, was always attentive to current projects in his shop. Since most of his men lived at the Stuttgart facility, work often went on around the clock.

As reported in Walter Henry Nelson's *Small Wonder*, "The three [NSU] prototypes vanished until 1950 when one of them unexpectedly reappeared in Stuttgart, driven by a crippled German war veteran who was a former NSU engineer. It survived the war and postwar years in the deserted Friedrichsruh Castle of the Hohenlohes near Ohringen." It was found by this veteran in 1948, bought for nearly nothing and brought back to his home. There he repaired the headlights and replaced the battery to find that the car ran like new.

four-wheeled vehicles because it competed directly with the popular Fiats of the time.

In place of the Type 32, NSU decided instead to make a low-cost "people's motorcycle" called the NSU Quickly. This was a crushing blow to Porsche. Once again, he had developed a car through the prototype phase only to be denied a chance to put it into production. Because of the lack of completed projects and the fact none of his previous designs had reached the production stage, 1934 was becoming a financially and emotionally frustrating time for the design studio and its 23-person staff.

2

Hitler and His "People's Car"

Porsche presented Hitler with this scale model, which Hitler greatly admired. Although Porsche disagreed with his political views, Hitler supported him fully, which is the main reason the Beetle survived.

In 1923, while serving nine months of a five-year prison term in Landesberg jail for attempting to overthrow the German federal government in the infamous "beer hall putsch," Adolf Hitler did two things: 1) he wrote *Mein Kampf*, and 2) he read a biography of Henry Ford. Both proved inspirational because, 10 years later, when the Nazi party had swept into power, one of Hitler's propaganda ideas to bolster support for his regime was to provide a car for the everyday man. In *Mein Kampf*, he wrote of "breaking the motoring privileges of the upper classes." He believed that if he improved the social status of the common worker, he would be regarded as a great leader. Hitler felt that the world regarded a country's power by the growth of its auto industry, and

at the 1933 Berlin Auto Show, he explained that a nation is no longer judged by its miles of railroad tracks but by its miles of paved highways. He promised that all German citizens would own a car in as little as 10 years. Furthermore, he promised to lower car taxes, build a vast network of roads and highways, lighten the then stringent motorists laws and make it easier for all people obtain licenses.

Hitler enjoyed automobiles, though rarely ever drove himself. It is rumored that he never learned to drive, but it isn't proven. He knew that the potential ownership of a car, especially in the Depression-swept 1930s, would be a powerful incentive to his citizens that he could use to manipulate them.

At the 1934 Berlin Auto Show, he sealed

his promise by saying: "It is a bitter thought that millions of good and industrious people are excluded from the use of a means of transport that, especially on Sundays and holidays, could become for them a source of unknown joy." This became an increasing popular and useful tool to garner much needed support.

Early in 1933, Hitler made it known that funds would be available for racing projects, provided the right companies bid for the positions. Daimler-Benz, which had been making and racing cars for many years, enjoyed a successful and proven track record and was deemed a favorite of the new Chancellor. When Porsche heard that there was close to 600,000 marks of government funds available, he quickly convinced infant carmaker Auto Union (a company that formed in 1932 by combining Wanderer, Horch, Audi and DKW) to bid for the project. Porsche's designs met with the Auto Union board's approval, and in May 1932, Baron Klaus D. von Oertzen, board member for the new Auto Union company, asked Porsche to accompany him to Berlin to help sell the proposal to Adolph Hitler.

Hitler had met Porsche briefly almost 10 years before, at the Solitude race near Stuttgart. They had been introduced by the then press chief of Daimler-Benz, Dr. Völter. Being a fan of racing and the designs of Porsche, Hitler remembered the meeting, although Porsche didn't. After the formalities were concluded, Hitler frankly declared that Porsche and his partners suggestion that their company could rival that of the mighty Daimler-Benz was simply outrageous. At this point, Porsche reportedly stepped in and spoke for nearly half an hour about the benefits of Auto Union's proposed design. He spoke of the rear-mounted engine just in front of the rear axles, the new torsion bar and trailing arm suspension, the advanced design of the V-16 engine and the advantages of these components on the track.

Hitler was impressed with Porsche after the meeting, so much so that the funding was split between Daimler-Benz and Auto Union. Porsche's design, a 600hp, 16-cylinder Grand Prix car, went on to win three Grand Prix races in 1934, and the respect of Adolf Hitler and the racing world. Hitler was an avid race fan and automobile enthusiast. His plan to put every man in to a car in as little as 10 years provided him and the Nazi party much needed support in the early years. In order to make this seemingly impossible dream a reality, Hitler needed a car designer in Germany to create the "people's car," and quickly.

Jakob Werlin

Jakob Werlin was a Mercedes dealer in Munich. His first claim to fame was that he sold Adolf Hitler his first Mercedes in 1923, at a time when the Nazi Party was struggling with its finances. Despite the cost, Hitler argued that the 60 hp Mercedes was a much needed tool to visit the growing Nazi rallies in various parts of the country.

Because of this relationship, Hitler often turned to Werlin for advice on all things automotive. Hitler knew he had to fulfill his pre-election promise of delivering a car for all people, so he approached Werlin and convinced him to speak with the Daimler-Benz board to see if they would build a car for him and his country.

Of course, this being 1932, Hitler was not yet elected and Werlin was just a dealer, so the Daimler-Benz board rejected the idea. How things changed in little more than a year. Hitler became chancellor, and Daimler-Benz, realizing that Werlin had a relationship with Hitler, promoted him to the board of directors.

Timing, they say, is everything, and this is true of how the Beetle came to be. Just as Porsche was putting the finishing touches on his Auto Union Grand Prix car in 1933, he received word that NSU was no longer interested in a small car, leaving Porsche and his design team wondering if they would ever live to see the "VolksAuto" on the road. Soon thereafter, Jakob Werlin was in the neighborhood of the Porsche headquarters in Stuttgart and decided to pay Porsche a visit, as he hadn't seen him since their days together at Daimler-Benz five years before.

Porsche was quite suspicious of Werlin's motives at first. He believed Werlin was looking for inside information on his rear-engine racecar, which was directly competing with the racecars from Daimler-Benz. So, he spent much of the time discussing his talking about his designs for a people's car. Werlin realized that he might have found Hitler's solution to his promise to deliver a "people's car." Werlin suggested to Porsche that he draw up his ideas in writing and be prepared to voice his opinions to Hitler himself.

Kaiserhof Meetings

The paper Porsche put together was called "Ideas on the Construction of a German People's Car," and on January 17, 1934, Porsche presented his paper to Werlin, Hitler and the Ministry of Transportation.

In this document, Porsche suggested that the cars on the market were of a high quality but with prices beyond the reach of average income. Although the price of the "people's car" must be low, the high standard of quality must not be compromised in any way. He wrote:

"A people's car should not be a small car which perpetuates the tradition of previous products in this range by simply exactly copying their pattern with reduced dimensions, power, weight and so forth. A vehicle such as this might be cheap in terms of its purchase price, but from the point of view of a healthy national economy, it would be of little value because of its reduced passenger comfort and life span, and therefore in the long term, it would be anything but cheap.

"1) A people's car should not be a small car whose dimensions are reduced at the expense of handling and life expectancy, while it remains relatively heavy; instead, it should be a functional vehicle of normal dimensions but relatively low weight, a goal that can be achieved by fundamentally new processes.

"2) A people's car should not be a small car with limited power at the expense of maximum speed and good climbing ability, but a fully practical vehicle which has the necessary power to achieve normal maximum speeds and climbing capability.

"3) A people's car should not be a small car with reduced passenger space at the expense of comfort, but a fully functional vehicle with normal, comfortable space within its bodywork.

"4) A people's car should not be a vehicle with limited uses, but should be able to fulfill all conceivable purposes by simple exchange of bodywork, for use not only as a passenger vehicle but as a commercial vehicle and for certain military purposes.

"5) A people's car should not be fitted with complex equipment requiring increased servicing, but should be a vehicle with as far as possible foolproof equipment, to reduce servicing to an absolute minimum.

The following qualities are demanded of the car:

The best possible suspension and handling
A maximum speed of about 60mph
Closed four-seat bodywork for the transport of passengers
The lowest possible purchase price and running costs."

Based on a set standard of requirements he had worked out by his involvement in two previous projects and years of contemplation, he devised a list of specifications:

Track: 1200mm
Wheelbase: 2500mm
Maximum Power: 26bhp
Maximum Engine Speed: 3500rpm
Curb Weight: 650kg
Selling Price: 1550 marks
Maximum Speed: 60mph (100km/h)
Climbing Ability: 30 percent
Fuel Consumption: 35mp
Chassis Design: Full Swing Axle

Porsche concluded his report by saying, "The construction of the people's car is especially close to my heart; all sections of the population have great expectations of this vehicle." In May 1934, Werlin phoned Porsche and requested that he meet with him and Hitler at the Kaiserhof Hotel in Berlin to discuss the "KleinAuto" idea and fetter out any remaining details and requirements both parties may have. The following day, Porsche was greeted by Werlin and Hitler, and they all sat down for tea.

At first glance, on the surface of casual conversation, the two men had much in common. They both were Austrian, coming from similar small towns and likewise quiet, modest upbringings. They both despised the elite and wealthy industrialists of Germany, championing the common man. Porsche was bitter because of his previous employers' lack of enthusiasm for his small-car projects, and Hitler was bitter simply because most of the wealthy industrialists were Jews. Because of their backgrounds and interests in auto racing, they had much to talk about, as they had many mutual acquaintances and shared similar stories of races they had both seen. Despite Porsche's aversion to politics, the two got along splendidly and spoke throughout the evening. Porsche outlined his plans, explaining that 1430-lbs. vehicle should have four-wheel independent suspension and capable of achieving 100km/h. Hitler interjected his thoughts and concerns. He didn't want the car just capable if reaching 100km/h, but he wanted the car to cruise comfortably at that speed. Furthermore, he suggested that the car's engine be aircooled. The only drawback is that Hitler insisted that the price for the car be below 1000 marks, about the price of a medium sized motorcycle at the time.

As much as Porsche disagreed on the price, the idea of a chance to build his dream car was too big to pass up. After all, if he couldn't get the chancellor of Germany to build his car, who would?

Of course, with a project of this magnitude, and especially that it involved a government entity, there were drawbacks. And even in Hitler's circle of influence and realm of power, there was red tape to be cut and obstacles to be overrun. For example, after Porsche presented Hitler with the prototype plans and the approval was granted, he met resistance with the German Automobile Industry Association, a board of directors, per se, that had the power to decide whether or not Porsche's prototypes would be allowed into production or not. The RDA (Reichsverband der Deutsche Automobilindustrie) had no interest seeing a governmentally funded car damage the profitability of their own manufacturers. So they ordered Porsche to produce three prototypes and have them ready for review in 10 month's time, a seemingly impossible task designed to foil his attempts.

However, after the designs were finished and the prototypes approved, where would the car be produced? This uncertainty ensured the proper cooperation of Germany's other carmakers and kept the expressed jealousy to a minimum. After all, who would be there if the whole project fell apart at the seems?

The contracts were signed on June 22, 1934, and he was to be paid approximately 20,000 marks (or $8000) a month for the project. The work began soon there after.

Ferdinand Porsche was lacking the proper equipment to build these cars, so his double garage in Stuttgart was cleared out and tools and workers brought in. As frustrating a situation this may have presented for the design team, Porsche was extremely elated. The Volkswagen was coming.

The Prototype 60

Given the green light, Porsche began work on a car that would resemble the Zündapp/NSU projects unfinished the year before. Porsche's home on Killesberg in Stuttgart soon became a hive of activity, as a dozen men, lathes, milling machines and other metalworking tools dominated the small space.

At the 1935 Berlin Auto Show, Hitler stalled for time as the prototypes were readied. But the optimism among the general public remained and was further fueled by Hitler's speech at the show's opener. He said: "I am so happy that due to the superb designer Porsche and his staff, we have succeeded in creating preliminary designs for a German people's car, so that the first models will finally be tested by the middle of this year." However, Hitler, Porsche and his staff knew well that the first models couldn't possibly be ready for testing by the middle of the year. They were quite a bit behind schedule, and Hitler was growing impatient.

V1 and V2

By April 1935, 10 months after he signed the contract, Porsche hadn't delivered the prototypes and it didn't look as though he would be able to do so any time soon. Despite the RDA's desire to kill the project so they could get back to healthy non-government-backed competition, Hitler stepped in and demanded that they allow an extension on the contract to give Porsche more time to complete the cars. The extension was obviously granted.

Meanwhile, in Stuttgart, month after month went by and Porsche and his staff still labored away. Porsche had gone through many changes to the designs since the initial plans had been approved by the RDA in

During an outing to the Black Forest in 1936, some of the Porsche family and employees stretch their legs next to the V2 and the V1. Standing near the V1 sedan is Ferry Porsche on the left.

1934. Most of the changes to the design were justified by expense, space and weight. The car was rear-engine, instead of front-engine like most all of the cars being produced during that time, because he didn't want to compromise passenger space by having a tunnel to house the driveshaft. Plus, tunnels and driveshafts added weight and expense to the bottom line. For example, it would cost additional time and money to have a machine to produce the tunnel, or bend the pan to fit the added shape. This was not economic and was immediately dropped from the design.

In his paper "Ideas on the Construction of a German People's Car," Porsche explained that the advantages of a rear-engine car allow for the, "unlimited use of the length of the vehicle, allowing favorable positioning of the seats; no intermediate shaft, hence low intrinsic weight; good accessibility and reparability; vibration-free positioning; no road noise or engine smell in the car." The fact that it is aircooled made sense to Porsche because watercooled engines were more expensive, requiring an expensive and heavy radiator and had the tendency to boil

Ferry Porsche at the wheel of the V2 Convertible. Notice the wheel/tire sizes, at 4.5x17, is much wider than the production version.

over in hot Germany summers and freeze up in cold Germany winters. Since the average German worker was without a garage to store the car in, most of them would spend much of their time sitting outside exposed to the elements. Plus, a watercooled car required additional parts (meaning additional designing), which equaled additional cost, construction and future repair. The only disadvantage with the aircooled design is that it is noisier, because it doesn't have the jacket of water surrounding the case to deaden some of the internal engine sounds.

The first three prototypes were labeled with type numbers (V1 and V2), similar to how they are labeled now, but as a group, they were called Type 60. The "V" stood for Versuch, which is the German word for experimental, and there were two types, Number One and Number Two.

The V1 closely resembled the Type 32 design he had wanted to use for the NSU project. It was a rear-engine, aircooled car with a torsion bar suspension. At the front, there were two tubes, and instead of one

tube containing twin torsion bars like on the Type 32 design, each tube contained one torsion bar. They were more compact, less expensive than leaf springs and easier to maintain, protected by the tube from harsh environments or a poorly kept road. The chassis, or floor pan, consisted of almost a single sheet of metal bent and shaped so much so that it provided much of the car's strength. However, the prototype was only a centralize steel tube with the floor constructed of plywood. The common method at the time was to construct a steel girder chassis and build a car on top of it, instead of combining the efforts of the body with that of the pan to provide the lightest, most cost-effective way of producing the same results.

The prototypes were first powered by a variation of the 1912 Austro-Daimler airplane engine Porsche had designed, mainly to keep costs down under the targeted 1000 marks per car. He also experimented with a two-cylinder, two-cycle, watercooled engine that proved to be unfit for long distances. Next, Porsche tried an aircooled, four-cylinder, two-cycle engine but it had too little power to fit the requirements. Even a three-cylinder radial engine was considered. Finally, a 33-year-old designer, Franz Reimspeiss, discovered the solution: an engine that would be the heart for millions of Volkswagens to come: the aircooled, four-cylinder, four-cycle engine. It was very similar to the one he designed for the NSU, cheaper than the two-cycle models and better suited for export to other countries. In all, 20 engines were designed, built, tested and deemed unfit before they settled on the Reimspeiss design.

The V1's body design is generally credited to Erwin Kommenda. The style reflected the trend of the European auto industry in the mid-1930s. Similar cars were being produced during this time, such as the Tatra, designed in neighboring Czechoslovakia by Hans Ledwina. The Tatra had an aircooled rear-engine design and the sleek, streamlined body style bore a striking resemblance to later Volkswagen prototypes. This is mainly because the Tatra factory was taken over by Germany in 1938, and no doubt the auto designs were shared with German auto manufacturers.

Considering the lack of floor space to properly construct each car, the prototypes were built side-by-side in Porsche's garage. The V2 Cabriolet was given a folding canvas top, with similar appearance to the V1, aside from the top. The headlights were still mounted in the nose, and rear-hinged doors opened to a spartan interior. There was a fuel tank under the hood of each Versuch and the rather thin tires were 4.5 inches by 17 inches.

The German car market was beginning the feel the impact of Hitler's little car, as many of them, Opel and Auto Union for example, began to reduce the prices of their cars. With the anticipation of the new government-produced cars, potential consumers were saving their money for when they were finally released. This was met with opposition from Hitler himself, who ordered that no car manufacturer would set the price of his cars to be in competition with that of the Kleinauto. With that said, the RDA approved the V1 and V2 prototypes, granting permission and funding to continue with the project by authorizing a further three prototypes to be built, the "VW3 Series."

V3

The 1936 V3 prototypes more closely resemble the VW Beetle most of us know today. Though still several design steps away from the final product, the overall shape and function of the V3 was completed. Several aspects were hanging over from the first prototypes, items such as suicide doors, no rear window and only the top half of the front hood was designed to open. The headlights were positioned nearer the fenders this time (instead of more centered on the hood), and they were lower and appeared more bulbous, set off from the fenders.

The first car of the V3 series is ready to begin extended testing by June 1936. Inside is a new steel floor instead of the wooden floors of the first two prototypes.

From the front, the V3 still has a double-latched hood and suicide doors.

At first, because of the constant pressure to keep costs low, Porsche designed the final product to be made of a wooden body frame covered with thin sheet metal. After considering the harsh German climate, the wood was dropped and a full steel shell employed instead. However, two of the three V3 prototypes were produced this way, while the other one was constructed completely of steel.

Testing the V3s

Though two of the V3s were ready on the

The chassis of the V3 had a steel floor pan, installed because it was hoped it would hold up better in Germany's harsh winters.

The interior of the V3 was simple and functional, not luxurious by any means. A simple dash, minimal padding for the seats and a basic floor covering kept costs down as much as possible.

projected deadline of June 1936, they weren't finally delivered until October 12 and 13 of that year. Though Porsche and his design bureau had already tested the first two for approximately 3500 miles together, the real testing by the RDA was just beginning.

Since there were only the three cars, the two-man teams from the RDA (one team for each car and two teams per car, per day) were instructed not to excessively abuse them. In case of a potential problem, the three vehicles were equipped with a wide variety of spare parts and tools to fix anything that may happen along the pre-determined routes. The cars covered a daily 435-mile test run, covering a wide variety of terrain from steep grades in the Black Forest during the morning to high-speed endurance runs along the newly constructed Autobahn between Stuttgart and Bad Nauheim.

During the entire testing phase, each of the three cars covered approximately 30,000 miles in mostly low-temperature winter weather and were closely monitored by the staff. Although there was no night testing, each car ran continuously six days a week. Every aspect of the car was evaluated, noted, commented upon and inspected by the two-man crews. By January 1937, a full report was compiled and released by the RDA. The most complained-about problem that was experienced with the V3 was the weak crankshaft, which caused considerable problems due to its cast-iron construction. It was replaced by a forged crankshaft, which the VW engine has used ever since. Electrical fuel pumps caused some malfunction and were replaced with mechanical ones, and the brakes and front suspension were criticized as well. More specifically, there were individual problems with each car, such as car Number One's gearshift breaking and the wheels wobbling after only 500 miles. On the second and third cars, the mechanical brakes gave out twice, once at 13,000 miles and again 3000 miles later.

At night, the crew at the Porsche factory

Daimler-Benz was now in charge of producing enough test subjects to satisfy the DAF (Deutsche Arbeitsfront), the government worker's union. The new series was called the VW30 and were produced in 1937.

After the bodies were made, they were mated up with the chassis at the Porsche shop in Stuttgart. There are slots in front of the door handles for the turn-signal semaphores.

put the cars back together in time for the next day's testing. They followed the three cars and the RDA staff around each day and made some notes of their own. According to Walter Henry Nelson's *Small Wonder*, the cars had problems even when they were running well: "One car ran into a truck, another into a motorcyclist, and once a car hit a large deer at full speed."

Overall, the three V3s fared well despite these problems and they concluded their testing two days before Christmas. The man responsible for the testing and evaluating the Volksautos, as they were now being called by the German and U.S. press, was Wilhelm Vorwig, the head of RDA's technical department. Needless to say, the members of the RDA hoped that Vorwig, one of their own, would find something wrong with the cars so the project could be cancelled. But Vorwig did his duty without bias and reported what he saw, although he did note once, "The sound of a crankshaft breaking," he said, "is enough to turn you pale."

In his extremely factual report, however, he offered few personal judgments and opinions on the car's future. Vorwig suggested that further testing be considered on a larger

scale. One thing he did mention was that he felt it would be a good idea to manufacture the car under better conditions and in the factories of the RDA members...not Porsche's garage at home.

VW30

Hitler's legendary paranoia entered the picture at this point. Hitler was convinced that there was a conspiracy to take the Volksauto away from Germany and have it manufactured in the U.S. He deeply distrusted the RDA and its head, Wilhelm von Opel, whose company was backed partly by the American automaker Ford. Hitler's patience for the project had grown thin, thanks in part to continued criticism from the various automakers in Germany and the RDA in general. So Hitler decided to remove the project from the RDA and shift the development to the German labor front, the DAF (Deutsche Arbeitsfront), headed by Nazi Dr. Robert Ley. Since trade unions were ruled illegal, the funds for these organizations were seized and channeled through the DAF to the Volkswagen project. Additional funding came from a 1.5 percent

The interior view of the completed driver's side. On the dashboard, next to the wheel is a temperature gauge to record the temperature during the severe testing phase.

The second completed VW30 is being pushed by workers out of the Daimler factory doors.

income tax on all DAF workers in Germany (every worker in Germany was a member!).

The DAF was overseen by a newly established and separate Nazi entity, the Gessellschaft zur Vorbereitung des Volkswagen (Society for the Development of the Volkswagen), known by its nickname

Gesuvor. This move gave full priority to the Volkswagen project, and allowed Hitler and his men to keep absolute control over the production of the prototypes. This organization was headed by Ley's assistant Dr. Bodo Lafferentz, and on May 28, 1937, Gesuvor received a transfer from DAF for approximately 500,000 marks.

More importantly, Porsche was no longer burdened by financial problems, and he could freely concentrate on the design and development. The next step was more testing, as Vorwig had suggested, so the DAF provided funding for 30 prototypes for testing. Porsche set to work creating the first of this limited production run in his Stuttgart garage. The remaining 29 cars, built to his specifications, were reluctantly produced by Daimler-Benz. Daimler-Benz was smart enough to realize that declining the order would not be in its best interests, and proceeded to build a car that they felt would ultimately become a direct competitor.

It is interesting to note that each of the 30 prototypes was given its own special identification plate during the testing period. The first car, the one built at the Porsche Bureau, was numbered 111A-37000 and each successive car was given the next number in the sequence through 111A-37029.

The VW30s were not fitted with bumpers, so they had a very streamlined appearance. The fenders now held the headlights, instead of the front apron, and the car looked more Beetle-like than ever. The missing rear window, suicide doors and awkward front hood remained. Changes included increased output of the flat-four engine, drum brakes on all four corners, and the tires were upgraded to Continentals (4.60x16in.).

The test period officially began April 1, 1937 and didn't conclude until December 31, 1937. During this time, the 30 cars traveled a combined total of approximately 800,000 miles. They were broken into several groups for specialized testing programs that consisted of city driving, country and

Side by side, the two cars, the VW30 on the left and the older V3 on the right still have a remarkable similarity, aside from the smallest details.

The VW30 was equipped with a four-speed transmission.

This rear view of the VW30 drivetrain, with the engine bolted to the transmission, was tested for over a million miles. Notice the ignition coil mounted on the back of the fan housing.

mountain terrain, and highway speed tests. Men from the elite German SS troops were brought in to participate in the testing. These men all had military training and experience with driving and testing automobiles, and the cars were transported to the SS tank barracks at Kornwestheim to allow for a regimented schedule of rigorous testing. This level of extreme testing was relatively unheard of at this point in time, and the results allowed few doubts that the Volkswagen was to become a rugged and reliable little car. It had proven itself mechanically, but the overall look and style needed modification.

What remained to do was for Porsche's main body designer, Erwin Kommenda to develop the body further. He came up with the basic shape of the classic Beetle that

Ferdinand Porsche designed and patented the torsion bar suspension with the lightweight people's car in mind. It was royalties from this patent that helped finance him through the lean years of the early '30s.

21

With simple lines and graceful curves, the VW30 resembles the basic design that would stand for decades.

The VW30 has a louvered engine cover for enhanced cooling. For the next series of prototypes, this was the first thing to go.

Each VW30 was rigorously tested for several months and many thousands of miles. Shown here on the road to Zell em See, this VW30 tests its high attitude skills.

Testing also was conducted on city streets, where the unusually shaped VW30s usually attracted quite a bit of attention. This woman appears not to notice, however.

would endure for the next 50 years. The doors were altered so that they opened from the rear, and the front hood was stamped from a single piece of sheet metal, instead of two. Most importantly, two pieces of thin glass, shaped like beans were placed in the back as the rear windows. Cooling louvers were added above the engine lid and hub caps were the final touches.

VW38 and the KdF-Wagen

Named the VW38 series, a final run of 44 prototypes were built, however, the car didn't even have a name yet. The prototypes, tested to the extreme limits of their ability, were dubbed KdF-Wagens, which stood for Kraft durch Freude or strength through joy, by Hitler himself. KDF was a division of the DAF that provided the funding for the car as well as a new factory. Hitler wanted to build an unheard of 1.5 million cars a year, so he needed an impressive factory. However, the name KdF-Wagen would only be a tempo-

Standing next to his personal VW30 that was given to him by his Uncle Ferdinand is Herbert Keas, Porsche's long-time engineer and son of his sister-in-law.

Storage was always a problem for the VW30 prototypes while they were on the road, so the engineers used whatever facility they could. Here, they are housed in the tank barracks at Kornwestheim during one break between test runs.

rary name until the end of the war.

For many years, Hitler had promised his citizens a people's car, and it looked as though he was finally going to deliver— almost. The DAF was having problems with funding in order to begin production. There was also the matter that not every German could afford to purchase the car, which was its intended purpose.

On August 1, 1938, Robert Ley proposed a solution to making the car more affordable. He suggested a savings plan for all citizens. Each person must purchase a savings booklet and add a minimum one five-RM stamp to it. When the person collected RM990 worth of stamps, he or she could trade the book in and drive away with a new Volkswagen. Of course, this didn't include the RM50 delivery charge or the RM200 to cover the first two years of insurance, not to mention accessories like a radio or a roll-back sunroof, but it covered the initial purchase of the car.

The plan seemed like a bargain, even though there was a non-cancellation clause, no interest on the initial investment and no guarantee of a delivery date. But by the end

The VW38 and later the VW39 (as they were called because they were produced in those years) were constantly on display. The KdF-Wagens were being displayed with the hopes that more people would join the savings plan to purchase one.

Citizens were given ample opportunity to inspect the KDF-Wagens, as they were on display all over the country. The idea was to encourage them to join the savings plan.

A rear shot of the KdF-Wagen shows the trusty flat-four.

The cover of the now famous 32-page KdF-Wagen savings booklet, enticing all to sign up for the KdF stamp program. Participants were required to purchase a five mark stamp each week.

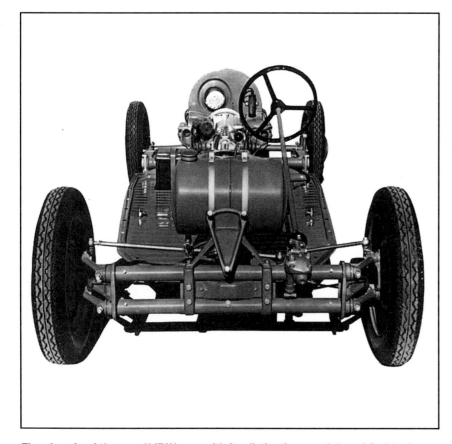

The chassis of the new KdF-Wagen with its distinctive round, barrel fuel tank.

of World War II, exactly 336,638 people had invested RM267 million into the German Worker's Bank. Of course, not a single person ever received his car because of the collapse of the German economy after the war. It wasn't until 1960 that Volkswagen settled with nearly 80,000 people who had filed a class action lawsuit. These people received a credit of 660 Deutsche marks (as the currency was now called), toward a new Beetle (priced around DM4000).

Hitler gives his speech at the ceremony marking the laying of the new factory's cornerstone, May 26, 1938. Hitler again promised that all citizens would be able to own his new People's Car, which he called the KdF-Wagen.

AutoStadt and the VW Factory

With the savings plan in place, work could begin on the factory. This was in early 1938. Designed by Peter Koller, the factory was officially called Stadt des KdF-Wagens (Strength Through Joy Car City) or simply AutoStadt. Known as Volkswagenwerks to the general public and the media, it was designed to be the largest automobile plant in the world, the centerpiece of a new town where 90,000 plant workers and their families would live once the plant was in full production.

Dr. Bodo Lafferentz, head of Gesuvor, was responsible for selecting the site. After scouting much of the country by air, he finally narrowed down his choice to some large fields outside of Fallersleben, a small town located about 25 miles from Brunswick in Lower Saxony. The location was ideal for several reasons. First, it was located in central Germany. The factory could be built directly on the Mittelland Canal, and the autobahn from Hanover to

With dignitaries and military officials looking on, the cornerstone is officially set in place by masons, who are wearing white suits and top hats.

Across the canal from the new factory, an entire town was being built to house the workers and their families. It was called KdF-Stadt, or simply Autostadt.

After an initial delay where workers were required to build a wall along the famous Maginot Line, construction continued on the factory, and it quickly began to take shape. The curved roofs held skylights that not only illuminated the factory floor during the day, but also saved energy costs by reducing the amount of electric light needed.

The new VW38 series was produced in 1938 and featured many refinements from the previous VW30 series, including a front hood that opened completely, a split rear window, running boards and bumpers.

Berlin was nearby. It was also a beautiful place to live and work.

The land was owned by Count von der Schulenburg, whose family had owned it since it was awarded to them in 1135 by Emperor Lothar II. Needless to say, he wasn't eager to sell it, but the pressure from Hitler finally prevailed.

In addition to the assembly line, Koller's final plans called for a power plant, a rubber and glass factory as well as a proving grounds for testing.

On May 26, 1938, Hitler visited the factory's future site for the cornerstone dedication. Attended by over 70,000 people, Hitler used this chance to promote the growing Nazi regime, and since the people's car was to be a part of that revolution, he made use of the situation.

Though his mind was visibly preoccupied with the annexation of Austria that only occurred the previous week, he still managed a rousing speech that, in short, declared to the people that the car was "to bring joy" to all. This joy never came, however; two days after the cornerstone dedication, he invaded Czechoslovakia.

One month later, construction of the plant

was abruptly halted, as most of the contractors and workers were ordered to help build the "West Wall" fortifications that faced France's Maginot Line, known as the Siegfried Line. It would be two months until construction resumed and several years until the factory was completed, though 124 KdF-Wagens were built at the Daimler-Benz plant, and sold to high-ranking Nazi officials. It was at this time, during the Berlin Auto show of 1939, the little car was given its official nickname, the Volkswagen. Although the car was officially called the KdF-Wagen, the news media and public picked up this unofficial moniker instead. The Volkswagen, at the time, was a common reference to any small car made for mass production in Europe.

Ferdinand Porsche points out some of the technical details of the three V303s to Hitler after his speech. On Porsche's lapel is the commemorative cornerstone laying pin.

This is the V303 series convertible. After the ceremony, Porsche drove Hitler to the train station in this car.

The Beetle Goes to War

3

Journalists are given a glimpse of the KdF-Wagens during the 1939 Berlin Auto Show.

Just as the production of the Beetle was to start in 1939, the Reich Air Ministry realized it was much more important to utilize the factory to support the war effort than to build Volkswagens, which were of little use on the battlefield in their present form. Therefore, the Volkswagenwerk was placed under the authority of the German air force and commissioned to tailor its production line to manufacture two variations of the Kdf-Wagen that would be more suited for battle—the Kübelwagen, followed by the Schwimmwagen.

During Hitler's military buildup, all able-bodied men were drafted to fight in the war, which included many of the employees of the Volkswagenwerk. The factory was then staffed with those either unfit for war, or with political prisoners, refugees, and those too wounded to fight any longer.

Although the plant was operational, it was still not fully complete. Final construction of the plant and the city of Autostadt came almost to a halt when the Nazis began invading Europe. Building materials were scarce as most resources, including labor, were dedicated to supporting Hitler's enormous military buildup. By the end of 1941, only 10 percent of the housing complex at AutoStadt was complete with only 2358 apartments. Wooden barracks were hastily constructed instead and would be used by workers until the end of the war.

Many officials believed the war wouldn't last very long, so they were reluctant to convert the factory to build for the war at first. But when they finally did, the factory only operated at about 20–25 percent of its potential during 1940 to 1942. This weak production output was attributed to the fact that Volkswagenwerk, the most modern auto-making facility in the world, was splintered into many different departments producing many different types of war-related equipment, machinery and munitions. There was a considerable lack of organization and management; quite often, one part of the factory had no idea what the other was doing.

By 1944, every auto manufacturer in Germany offered at least one vehicle for military use, which added some confusion and cost when it came to ordering vehicles and parts. The military had long wanted to standardize their vehicles, but had not been able to reach a decision. Despite the enthusiasm for the new Volkswagen design, the Wehrmacht officials were pressured by other auto manufacturers, who had become dependent on the military to keep their companies going. Not many citizens were buying cars at this time for obvious reasons. If a state-run factory was to become the sole provider of military transportation, the economic impact would be devastating to companies such as Daimler. These companies were able to hold off such a decision until early 1944, when Hitler finally decreed that Porsche's Kübelwagen become the official car of the German army.

The Kübelwagen

The origins of the Kübelwagen can be traced to as early as 1934, when Porsche's team was asked to adapt the proposed "People's Car," for military use. Franz Reimspiess, who designed the timeless VW symbol still used today, designed an all-terrain vehicle based on the KdF-Wagen.

In 1940, Adolf Hitler visited Fallersleben and the VW factory to see the progress of Porsche's Kübelwagen and other war machines. Pictured here are Porsche (in the hat) Jacob Werlin and Dr. Robert Ley. Werlin is at far left, with Ley next to Porsche.

Hitler being personally guided through an unknown part of the factory, still under construction, in 1940.

Called a Type 62, it had 19-inch wheels, very little bodywork and no doors or roof. This "rough draft" was rethought by Porsche the following year and a new prototype was made—Type 82.

It was a strange-looking vehicle, first

Hitler and Porsche discuss the KDF and other projects under development.

Dr. Bodo Lafferentz (right) and Porsche (center) admire the Kdf-Wagen.

These four KdF-Wagens were to be awarded to various officials, indicated on the license plates. From left to right: Dr. Bodo Lafferentz, Professor Porsche, Gauleiter und Reichsstatthalter Otto Telschow, head of all annexed territorial governments of Poland and Austria. The first KdF-Wagen produced (far right with an unidentified nameplate and a center cowl-mounted aerial bearing the swastika) was rumored to be given to Hitler.

called the Kübelsitzwagen (bucket-seat car), but later shortened to Kübelwagen. It was first produced on December 21, 1940. One thousand were made before the end of that year, and by the close of the war, almost 50,000 had rolled off of the assembly line and onto the front lines. Before 1943, the car featured a 985cc engine that generated 22.5 horsepower, giving the vehicle a maximum speed of 80kph. The bodies were made by

Ambi-Budd in Berlin, shipped to Fallersleben and the chassis were assembled in one part of the Volkswagenwerk. It featured a folding windshield, a canvas top and four doors, with the front pair hinging at the back so they could swing on a common post with the rear doors. A shovel, spare tire/wheel and black-out light were mounted directly on the hood, under which there was no storage space aside from a spare five-gallon fuel tank that slid into place behind the pedals.

Ingeniously designed, the rear light cluster was geared for wartime with a green plastic cover that had differing thickness. This enabled a driver in a following car to judge the distance to the car ahead by how many lights were visible. The interior was spartan to say the least. Covered in lightly padded canvas, the seats were uncomfortable during long drives, while the rear seat was simply a bench. Between the seats stood gun mounts for the occupants. Its aircooled engine could withstand the sauna-like heat of Africa and the bitter cold of Russia. Thanks to Porsche's son Ferry, the drivetrain included a gear-reduction system at the end of each swing axle so the vehicle could drive at a walking pace for parades and troop move-

Unidentified military and civilian officials, on December 20, 1940, stand next to the 1000th Kübelwagen produced. More than 50,000 followed.

Further back in the production line, Kübel bodies meet Beetle running gear in the final building stages.

Kübelwagen bodies were produced by the Berlin military coach builder Ambi-Budd, then taken to the VW plant for final assembly.

ments—a system which resurfaced years later on the Microbus.

As General Rommel advanced deeper into the deserts of North Africa, Porsche designed a special model for use in the hot, sandy environment. It featured protected electrical systems, extra cooling equipment and a larger air filter—not to mention balloon tires for sand crawling. Unfortunately for the Nazis, a miscommunication sent these special Kübels to the freezing Russian front, forcing Rommel to make do with ordinary Kübels, which obviously were prone to breakdown. Even with the lesser models, he still wasn't disappointed with their performance.

A captured Kübelwagen, for example, was returned to England and dismantled for inspection, where the researchers discovered more than 100 lbs. of sand lodged in the bodywork—and it still drove strong. In March 1943, Porsche returned again to the drawing board and redesigned the Kübelwagen to satisfy the changes made by Party officials. He boosted horsepower to 25, increased engine displacement to 1130cc, redesigned the body and increased its road clearance.

The Schwimmwagen

In 1940, another vehicle was developed based on the KdF-Wagen. The Schwimmwagen prototype, then coded Type 128, was an amphibious vehicle with a top land speed of 80kph and a top water speed of 9kph. Its purpose was to be a new scout vehicle, and 30 of these were built at the Volkswagen plant and delivered to the Army's Pioneer (Engineer) units. It was further developed into a smaller, faster model and was pro-

Also designed by Porsche was the Schwimmwagen, an amphibious, four-wheel-drive vehicle that could travel on land as well as water. The Schwimmwagen was basically a bathtub on wheels with an outboard motor that was powered by the standard engine. A dog-leg gear drive activated the propeller.

The Type 166, shown here, was a smaller, lighter and more agile version of the Schwimmwagen's original Type 128 version.

duced for three years, from 1942 to 1944.

Coded the Type 166, the Schwimmwagen's production totaled 15,000, and it was 40cm shorter and 10cm wider than the Type 128. It was powered by the same 1130cc engine that was used in the 1943 version of the Kübel, yet proved to be stronger

all around. Issued mainly to the divisions of the Waffen-SS and the Wehrmacht Pioneer battalions, the new Schwimmwagen was also given to other elite troops, including reconnaissance units to replace their motorcycle sidecars.

The Schwimmwagen was a simple design

The Mittelland canal made for a convenient demonstration venue for the Schwimmwagen's capabilities. Since several versions and angles of this photo exist (both going in and coming out of the canal), perhaps this is a press introduction to the new body style.

but very popular among the troops, considering its extraordinary off-road capabilities coupled with its amphibious talents. However, it was not much more than a sealed tub on wheels with no doors and a rolled up canvas for a top. The exterior sported a blackout light, a paddle and a shovel. Above the hood was the exhaust system, which was located higher than the 128's and mounted horizontally across the width of the car. An obvious attachment was the externally mounted, three-blade propeller that hinged just below the rear-engine lid, which could be extended and raised as needed. The blade was surrounded by a metal shield to prevent bottoming and the housing was designed to break away from the coupling in case it was snagged in shallow water. The intermediate shaft, which was connected to the main driveshaft, engaged the propeller when it was in the down position. The upper shaft drove the lower shaft (which turned the screw) via a chain drive, and because of the direct link between the prop and the driveshaft, the speed could only be regulated by the gas pedal in one direction (no reverse).

The Schwimmwagen had two filler necks that reached separate fuel tanks with a combined capacity of 50 liters, while all other Volkswagens only had 40-liter tanks. Production was halted in 1944 because of costs and time management problems. Because of the confusion caused by the Allied advance, more resources were placed in other areas of the war effort, leaving the factory to be run by inept officers and managers.

VW Variations

From the original Volkswagen V1 prototype built in 1936, 58 different models were designed and built by the end of the war in 1945. Though most of these examples never made it past the prototype phase or the test

Volkswagen experimented with many variations of the Kübelwagen. With gasoline in short supply during the war, alternate fuel sources were tested and employed if possible. This Kübel is outfitted with a furnace that produced methane gas to power the vehicle.

The KdF-Wagen Kommandeurwagen is based on the four-wheel-drive chassis of the Kübelwagen and has bigger tires for better traction and a roller on the front to help ease it out of ditches. It was designed for Germany's Afrika Korps.

track, a few found their way into production. There were Kübelwagen delivery vans, pickups and scout cars, among others. Most notable was the Type 87, an all-wheel-drive Volkswagen that closely resembled today's VW in many ways. In later years, the Type 187 (called the Kommandeurwagen), would be built based on this model, a design that combined the Beetle body with the Kübel's high-riding chassis.

Like the 1943 Kübel, the opposed-piston engine of the Type 187 also generated 25 hp. Approximately 600 were manufactured for the Afrika Korps, modified to protect

Under the hood of the Kommandeurwagen sits a full-size spare tire on top of a flattened gas tank. In the spare-tire well is an extra fuel tank. The headlights are blacked out for wartime.

A map table was installed inside the Kommandeurwagen. Note the radio cut into the center console of the dash.

Charcoal is being fed into the front burner. Methane gas was produced from the charcoal and used as fuel for the engine.

against the dusty terrain common to North Africa. Balloon tires and rollers on the nose were installed to help the Kommadeur-wagen navigate rough terrain. After the defeat of the German army in Tunisia in May 1943, the remaining Type 187 vehicles were used in Europe.

The especially rough winter of 1941–42 prompted the government to contract Porsche to develop a car capable of operating in the snow. Porsche used a Schwimmwagen because of its smooth tub shape, and attached gripping tires built by the Rieger and Dietz firm. Unfortunately, the tires didn't have enough grip and spun too easily, getting the car stuck in snow. After that, designers turned their attention to building a track-driven vehicle, similar to a tank. They even tried replacing the front tires with skis. It's easy to see why the car never made it to production.

Type 164

Late in the war, a Type 82 Kübelwagen

was fitted with grooved tires, allowing it to be driven on railroad tracks. The wheels were matched to the width of a standard railroad track, then 1435mm.

The Porsche company was again contracted to create yet a another version of the Kübel, a six-wheeled vehicle. Designated Type 164, the cross-country vehicle was intended to be driven in both directions,

ZUM GEDENKEN AN TAUSENDE
VON ZWANGSARBEITERN UND
ZWANGSARBEITERINNEN,
DIE ALS RASSISCH UND PO-
LITISCH VERFOLGTE, ALS
KRIEGSGEFANGENE UND AUS
DEN VOM DRITTEN REICH
BESETZTEN LÄNDERN EURO-
PAS DEPORTIERTE IM VOLKS-
WAGENWERK FÜR DIE RÜS-
TUNGSANSTRENGUNGEN
UND DEN KRIEG EINES VER-
BRECHERISCHEN SYSTEMS
GELITTEN HABEN.

This plaque at the Volkswagen factory commemorates the slave labor that was used to not only build the factory, but to build the vehicles of war (including bombs, rockets and planes) during World War II.

Volkswagenwerks Narrowly Escapes Destruction

On April 8, 1944, Volkswagenwerks was hit with the first of four Allied bombing raids. More than 300 planes dropped over 3,200 bombs (with one bomber even crashing into the plant). Though the bombing destroyed nearly 30 percent of the factory and 20 percent of the machines, one bomb had the potential to destroy the entire the Volkswagen plant. It was dropped right between two giant power generators that supplied electricity to the factory and the neighboring town of Fallensleben. The bomb could have easily smashed both turbines, and along with it, all future ambition to restart the factory after the war. Power plants were hard-to-find in post-war Germany, and the factory would not have been able to operate without them. Fortunately, the bomb was a dud; it did not detonate, and the future of Volkswagen, although far from certain, was at least still alive.

have two steering wheels and two engines. The design never made it past the drawing board phase and in 1941 it was abandoned.

Even a dummy tank was constructed and fitted onto a Kübel frame. Though it was primarily built as a training vehicle for tank operators, it was also used in an attempt to fool the Allies. The panels that covered the wheels could be removed to imitate a scout car and the top turret was fitted with vision slits and could accommodate a small machine gun. Entry was through the top hatch in the turret. By 1945, with Germany on the verge of defeat, supplies to construct the Kübelwagens were scarce, and the need for them was quickly vanishing.

4

The British
Save the Beetle

The Volkswagenwerk landed in the British zone of occupation after the war. The British arrived at the factory (shown here before the end of the war) to find it barely operational, severely damaged, and without any leadership. Rather than shut it down, the British realized restarting the factory would be essential for restoring the local economy, providing much-needed jobs to nearby citizens.

It seemed that when Hitler and Nazi Germany died, so did the idea of producing a people's car for the common citizen. The Volkswagenwerk factory had been converted to churn out war machines, not cars, and had been heavily bombed as a result. But the administrative officers of Volkswagen refused to crumble. To them, the need for an affordable, reliable car for common citizens was greater than ever.

Because of the heavy damage to the Volkswagenwerk, production numbers obviously slipped to an all-time low. Production was further hampered by the lack of tooling and machinery. Near the very end of the war, Hitler had ordered that all machinery be removed from the plant and hidden in mine shafts in Longway on the Belgian border. But the first train carrying up to 200 machines was seized by the American army at the Belgian border. Fortunately, Porsche stopped any further shipments of machinery, otherwise the factory would have most certainly closed down.

However, when American forces finally marched into Germany in April, 1945, the troops did not occupy the city or the factory

Where is the engine? British officers inspect a KDF-Wagen. Many were seeing one for the first time, unaccustomed to a rear engine layout.

The Royal Corps of Electrical and Mechanical Engineers arrived and quickly got the plant running again. Thousands of refugees returned to Germany, desperate for work, and found it on the assembly line. Within two months, KDF-Wagens, officially renamed Volkswagen by the British, began rolling off the assembly line once again.

because they didn't know where it was, or that it even existed. Because the city was so new, Fallensleben or Volkswagenwerk didn't appear on any of their ground maps, although the Air Corps knew of the target. As the Americans neared, vital parts of the remaining machines were frantically packed into crates and hidden in the electrical conduit pipes under the factory floor. The Nazi army fled, leaving the mostly captive labor force to do as they pleased. Once they realized they were no longer prisoners, the

The normal front spindles were not available after the war, so Kübelwagen front axles were used. All of these Beetles ended up with high ground clearance because of this.

workers began looting the plant, destroying machinery, burning files and stealing anything that wasn't bolted down. The mob seized control of the factory, and threatened to burn down the town of Fallensleben as well. Antonius Holling, a Catholic chaplain assigned with the Nazi battalion that had guarded the plant, realized that something had to be done, and drove an abandoned ambulance to meet with the advancing American army.

The "army" he found consisted of just 11 men and one young lieutenant, who expressed no interest in occupying the city or the factory. Holling pleaded with him, mentioning that there were 20 American-born German children stranded in the city.

Whether this was true or not is uncertain, but the next day, two dozen Sherman tanks and 200 soldiers entered Fallensleben and restored order to the factory.

By May 1945, only one-third of the factory was operational, and in serious need of money, equipment and skilled labor. Germany had been split into four zones, each controlled by one of the four main Allied forces—France, the United States, Britain and Russia. Fortunately for the future of VW, the plant was in the British zone and under British control, and for the most part, they left the factory as is. Other factories in other zones were being dismantled and relocated, and anything that even closely resembled or had ties to the Nazi

Materials were difficult to get after the war so many completed vehicles were traded to companies in exchange for sheet metal to build more cars. Wartime brake lights were still being used until they were replaced with the "Pope's nose"-style lights.

regime was either renamed or destroyed altogether.

The British took over the plant in June of 1945. A corps of the Royal Corps of Electrical and Mechanical Engineers arrived at the plant and quickly set up a repair and maintenance shop in one corner of the factory. Because of anti-Nazi sentiments, they renamed the factory Wolfsburg Motor Works after a nearby 14th-century castle belonging to Count Werner von der Schulenberg.

The German workers who remained at the plant began to fix the machinery and even produced two complete cars under British control. The two cars (Type 87s—experi-

mental four-wheel-drive Kübelwagen chassis—similar to the more commonly known Beetle) were sent to the British Army headquarters for review. The British were so impressed with these two post-war examples that they ordered 5,000 more. This helped to jumpstart the factory.

With typical British efficiency, the first thing the British did was to introduce a model number system to correctly identify the various models. The old KdF-Wagen was the Type 1, the Kübelwagen was Type 2, and the Kübel chassis with the KdF-Wagen sedan body was the Type 5. In addition, there was a second digit that identified the actual body type: a sedan was number 1, a convertible was numbrer 2.

Only 522 Kübelwagens were produced between June and December 1945, because that is the total number of bodies Ambi-Budd, the main supplier, was able to produce. Soon thereafter, Ambi-Budd became part of the Russian zone and they were prohibited from supplying the car bodies. By February 1946, production of the Kübelwagen was stopped, and the 6,000 workers were left with almost nothing to do.

Refugees from all over gravitated to the plant, looking for work and food. The British were forced to deal with the problem of the vast number of refugees, but the plant was barely working. The British quickly came up with a solution. While making their way through Germany and other occupied territories, both the British and American armies had collected quite a few German vehicles of all kinds, many damaged or broken, but still salvageable. To keep the plant running and to provide work for all of the refugees, the British decided to use the facility to repair and maintain these light vehicles. This work was first overseen by British Colonel Michael McEvoy. McEvoy soon decided that the plant was capable of producing their own vehicles in-house with the equipment on hand. With Ambi-Budd no longer supplying the Kübelwagen bodies,

The plant was finally running again, but it lacked one major component: a true leader. Major Ivan Hirst, right, was sent by the British army to rebuild the factory and get it fully operational, with the long-term goal of returning it to the German people.

and because the Kübelwagen, which was built as a war machine wouldn't be needed anyway, the next obviously candidate for production was the KDF-Wagen. The British dropped the KdF-Wagen name, and instead officially called the little car "Volkswagen." (up until that point, Hitler and many others had referred unofficially to the little cars as "Volks Autos" or "Volkswagen," literally, people's cars or people's wagons, but the official name had always been KDF-Wagen.)

By the end of 1945, over 1,700 Volkswagens had been built. Although the factory had plenty of workers and demand was high, it was unable to produce more cars because of a shortage of materials. To alleviate this, a discreet bartering system to trade VWs for sheet metal was set up to supply the factory with enough raw materials to build the cars. A single Volkswagen could be traded for a load of steel that could keep the assembly line going for two weeks. But since this practice of trading cars for supplies was frowned upon by the British government in England, many Volkswagens began to mysteriously disappear, reported officially as "lost in delivery."

Major Ivan Hirst

In the middle of August 1945, after the plant had been occupied for nearly two months, Major Ivan Hirst arrived. He had seen his first Volkswagen in Normandy the year before, and liked what he saw. Hirst agreed with McEvoy: that the car manufacturer should do what it knows how to do best, which was to produce cars. Little did he know then, but he was about to change automotive history. Colonel C. R. Radclyffe was put in charge of production, and the Beetle soon began rolling off the assembly line in various forms.

Hirst was born in Yorkshire, England, and was trained as an optical engineer before entering the military. During the war, he managed a traveling tank repair workshop to support the troops as they made their way across Europe. He arrived at Volkswagenwerk at the age of 29. The fact that he spoke fluent German probably had much to do with his appointment.

Hirst organized the plant and saved it from certain failure a number of times. He organized the assembly line, repaired machinery, and got production flowing again. Although

After the war, Porsche fled to Austria, where he was put under house arrest. He was later arrested by French authorities and charged with treason, but was later acquitted.

his management of the company would only last until 1949, his contribution to the Volkswagen is extraordinary. Years later, in 1981, he would be honored at the ceremony marking the production of the 20 millionth Beetle, which took place in Mexico.

What Happened to Ferdinand Porsche?

During all of these events, Ferdinand Porsche was nowhere to be found. He had fled to Austria, where he was placed under house arrest "for his own safety." He had little or no knowledge of what had happened to the plant, his designs or his car. He assumed that all had been lost or would be repatriated by the Allies to German citizens.

In July of 1945, he was invited to Frankfurt in the American zone of occupation to undergo a series of interrogations with other members of the Nazi Party. He was held in Dustbin, an old castle, along

with Albert Speer, but it soon became obvious that Porsche had little to contribute on political matters. He was released and allowed to return to Zell am See, Austria, where he had a home.

During his drive back, he decided to visit his old company in Stuttgart. The building was occupied by U.S. forces and he was denied entry. Porsche was upset that he couldn't even visit his own studio (which in fact was no longer his), so he returned to Zell am See, setting up a shop to repair military vehicles. He also designed small farm wagons and wheel barrels.

While settled in as comfortably as possible, Porsche suddenly received notice to appear before the French forces in their zone of occupation, in Baden-Baden to be presented with an "interesting assignment." Ferry Porsche went instead of his father to check out what this meant, because by now Porsche senior was becoming increasingly

A momentous occasion, as the 1000th post-war Beetle was produced in March 1946. At the wheel is none other than Major Ivan Hirst.

cautious, and with good reason. Ferry reported that a French technical commission wanted him to design a People's Car for the French, something based on the Volkswagen chassis but with a redesigned body. Excited, Porsche headed to Baden-Baden in the French zone on November 16, 1945.

He was certain the Wolfsburg factory was destined for dismantling and concluded the Volkswagen would never be made. As it turned out, the French were interested in obtaining the plant, but wanted to produce a prototype that would work before the deal was struck and the plant relocated to French soil. Both Ferry and Porsche, along with Porsche's son-in-law, Anton Piëch met with the French to negotiate. After reaching an agreement, the three men were invited to stay the weekend at a nearby resort while French representatives considered their offer.

But there were others who were very much against the idea of a French-owned people's car, mainly French automakers. On December 15, 1945, French officers arrested the Porsches and Piëch, placing them in prison, charging them with treason and war crimes. The chief accuser was Jean Pierre Peugeot, head of France's most powerful automaker bearing his name. Like many Germans at this time, they were guilty until proven innocent. Peugeot, whose French factory was placed under the control of Volkswagen during Germany's occupation of France, charged them with a violation of the Hague Convention (which bars the poor treatment of prisoners of war), claiming that his workers were prisoners of war and mistreated.

Just when all seemed to be lost, Ghistlaine Kaes, Porsche's faithful secretary of British citizenship, showed up, fresh from a series of adventures that had him narrowly escaping death at the hand of three countries. First, he was captured by the Nazis (because he was British), and sent to the Eastern Front, where he was wounded by the Russians, and sent to a hospital in Denmark. When the British overran the country, they didn't believe he was English, so they turned him over the Danish freedom fighters. Seconds before execution for treason, he

Volkswagens were leaving the factory at a steady rate soon after Hirst took over. Here was a trainload headed to France.

was sent to prison. After a short time, he was released and then tried for treason for a second time, this time by the British.

Acquitted, he returned to Zell am See, searching for Porsche. Upon his arrival to Baden-Baden, he was asked by Lecomte to produce the Volkswagen designs or Porsche would be killed. Kaes returned to the British zone and was again arrested, questioned for a week straight and sent to prison without charges. By this time, Porsche was removed to Paris and held in the villa of Louis Renault until 1947. That spring, after Porsche had been consulted on a wide variety of technical concerns dealing with the Renault car, they were moved to the dungeon at Dijon, where they remained until August 1, 1947, when they were released on 500,000 francs bail each.

The time spent in the three prisons affected Porsche's health. After returning to Austria, Porsche visited the Wolfsburg factory in September 1950, where he spent the day talking with Heinz Nordhoff about the future of the little car. Shortly after his trip, his health declined. Though the French never returned his million francs, they did acquit him of any war crimes.

On his 75th birthday, on September 5, 1950, his close friends and family threw him a party. As he walked out to the parking lot at the end of the evening, he was greeted by the sight of dozens of Volkswagens and Porsches. Ferdinand Porsche died a few months later, on January 30, 1951.

THE VOLKSWAGEN TRAVELS ABROAD

After the war, a number of Beetles and military vehicles were smuggled out of Germany, some to the States, and there was quite a bit of interest in this very unusual looking car. Volkswagen by now had only four different models for the Beetle, but with the German economy still in recovery, they knew they'd have to find new customers to survive. A German worker had to work five times a long as his American counterpart to afford a new Beetle. And, the rest of Europe was recovering fast, with much of the public in need of a new car. An export plan was needed.

The famous designer of the Transporter, Dutchman Ben Pon, had been interested in securing the import rights for the Volkswagen since before the war. When production numbers began to rise again, his interest rose with it. In August 1947, Pon became the official Volkswagen importer for the Netherlands and received 56 cars.

Hirst's tenure at the plant was only temporary. The British wanted a full-time German replacement. Heinrich Nordhoff, who had previously worked for Opel, was hired to replace Hirst.

Here Colonel Charles Radclyffe signs documents giving ownership of the VW plant to the German government. A new era begins.

By the end of the year, the little car was selling in Denmark and Switzerland and its future looked bright. Unlike the cars sold in Germany, the export models were better trimmed with additional chrome bumpers and hubcaps. As well, each batch of export cars were accompanied by a collection of spare replacement parts. This policy was very popular and established a great deal of loyalty with customers.

With sales expanding into many countries, the future of the Beetle looked promising. But to bring it up to world-class levels would require extraordinary leadership. Hirst knew that he would soon be returning to England, so he searched for and found a suitable replacement, Heinrich Nordhoff, who had previously worked for Opel. Nordhoff began running the plant in January of 1948, although Hirst remained at the plant to represent British authority.

Eventually Nordhoff would lead Volkswagen to world-class status during his reign. In 1949, the British formally returned control of Volkswagen and the Wolfsburg plant over to the new Federal Republic of Germany. Confident of its post-war potential, Nordhoff stated: "We cannot build as many cars as mankind needs. But if the worse comes to the worse, the last car to be bought will be a Volkswagen."

So began a new era for Volkswagen.

When Nordhoff assumed control, he streamlined and improved production, increasing output. The 10,000th Beetle was not far behind.

Dr. Hermann Münch, a Berlin lawyer, was named the official custodian of the VW factory, although he really had no influence on the production of the Beetle.

March 4, 1950. The 100,000thl VW rolls off the line, a milestone unthinkable just a few short years earlier. Nordhoff is at left, with a white handkerchief in his breast pocket.

5

The Reign of Heinrich Nordhoff

Heinrich Nordhoff (seated, center) is surrounded by his staff. To his right is Hugo Bork, the future first chair of the factory committee (head of the union). Under Nordhoff's authority and Bork's leadership, the workforce would grow to tens of thousands.

Although many credit Major Ivan Hirst with rescuing the Beetle from the ashes of World War II, few would argue that the man most responsible for the Beetle's existence and legendary rise to world popularity is Heinrich Nordhoff.

Nordhoff was born in Hildesheim, Germany on January 6, 1899. After graduating from Berlin Charlotten-burg Technical University in 1927, he began his automotive career as an apprentice with BMW. He gradually moved over to work at Adam Opel AG in Russelsheim, where he would begin honing the leadership and business skills that would elevate him to the top of the automotive industry.

In 1930, Nordhoff visited the United States to study the techniques of mass automotive production, and by the time the war broke out, he was managing director of Opel's truck division at Brandenburg, the largest truck plant in Europe. This is where he remained until Hirst contacted him about running Volkswagen in late 1947. At first, Nordhoff wasn't exactly thrilled with the idea. The little car was, after all, a competi-

By the time Nordhoff took over fully from the British government in 1949, the factory was well equipped and capable of building most all of their own parts under one roof, without having to rely on outside suppliers. This photo shows the size of the huge Schuler presses that were used to create the body panels and exterior parts.

tor, and in his view a rather poor one at that. He was once quoted as saying that the Beetle was a "poor, cheap, ugly and inefficient thing," remarking that the engine made a "noisy death rattle." The Beetle was dismissed by some of his fellow colleagues as nothing more than a political device that Hitler used to gain popularity. They didn't believe that the car would do well in the world marketplace. Nevertheless, he and his colleagues followed the development of the Volkswagen Beetle with some interest, but always remained somewhat skeptical of its chances for success.

However, at the end of the war, the economy looked very uncertain. Nordhoff had been decorated several times by Hitler, which tarnished his reputation somewhat with the Americans, and since Opel was partially owned by General Motors, he had reason to feel insecure. When the offer came from the British to rebuild an entire company, he realized this might be in his best interests. No doubt too, the challenge of resurrecting the huge factory and basically rebuilding the VW brand name from scratch was a challenge that appealed to him.

After assuming control, Nordhoff quickly got to work, assessing what the British had done and applying what he had learned by observing America's assembly lines. Production costs were soaring, so his first move was to streamline the assembly line and reduce the number of parts used by cutting down on the number of different models the plant was producing. By the time he took over, the plant was producing four entirely different cars, requiring different chassis, engines, bodies, etc. Instead, he ordered that one engine and one chassis be used underneath a total of five different bodies. At this time, Wolfsburg had 7000 employees producing a total of 6000 cars a month.

Destination—America

The British and Nordhoff had already begun to export Beetles as early as 1948, when one quarter of the production was shipped off to other countries, mostly in Europe. Nordhoff had only been at the helm of VW since January, but he already knew that the key to VW's survival would be to introduce the car to the American market-

Despite the vast amount of automated machinery at the factory, much of the assembly work was done by hand.

Here 36-hp engines are being built for the 1954 models.

Toward the end of the line for the bodywork on these 1952 Split-Window Beetles, workers attach the rear fenders and perform some final welding on the rear clip.

place, which was in the middle of an incredible post-war boom. Therefore, when he heard that Henry Ford II would be visiting Cologne, Germany, in March of 1948, he arranged a meeting with him and with Ernest Breech, chairman of the board of the Ford Motor Company. Nordhoff said that the British actually were offering the entire Volkswagen company to Ford for free. Henry Ford thought for a moment then turned to Breech for his opinion. Breech replied: "Mr. Ford, I don't think what we're being offered here is worth a damn." Perhaps some of the most famous last words ever uttered.

Snubbed, Nordhoff then directed his energies toward making VW and the Beetle a dominant force in the German economy, and in a sense, carrying out Porsche's and Hitler's original vision, which was to produce a "people's car" that was within the economic grasp of every German citizen.

The timing was certainly right. The German economy was beginning to boom as well, thanks to the tremendous rebuilding effort by the Allied forces. As the German economy expanded, jobs were created, and thousands of Germans suddenly needed, and could afford, new transportation, especially the Beetle. Production doubled twice in two years to over 46,000 Beetles by 1949. In fact, Volkswagen soon found it difficult to keep up with demand, especially since the Beetle was now being exported to many different countries (although America was not yet one of them). Soon, there were waiting lists, prompting VW to issue an ad campaign that said, *"Es lohnt sich, auf einen Volkswagen zu warten."* (It's worth waiting for a Volkswagen."). But there was one goal that remained: the American market.

The Beetle Goes Deluxe

This would be a tough sell. America's car designs couldn't have been more different than the Beetle's. Detroit was churning out huge, flashy, big-fendered land yachts with miles of bright chrome (think Chevy Bel Air or Cadillac tailfins). The Beetle would have to be pretty unique, and much more attractive than the relatively spartan models produced for the home market. What was needed was a new model with a higher level of quality, comfort and luxury. Nordhoff's designers came up with the Deluxe Model (also referred to as the Export Model). It had glossier paintwork, alloy trim and chrome-plated hubcaps, bumpers and handles. The interior was much more luxurious, with plush, cushy cloth upholstery and a sporty two-spoke steering wheel. The dashboard was bright and inviting, transforming the Beetle into a serious contender. Although outfitted with grab handles and an inside light, the Deluxe Beetle's interior included an instrument panel, steering wheel and plastic control knobs still painted black. In 1950, the Deluxes were given an ivory-colored two-spoke steering wheel and a rectangular mirror. An optional clock could replace the gearshift diagram. Braking power was switched from cable brakes to hydraulic, the engine gained a heat riser and the gas tank grew to 10 gallons of capacity. With these simple enhancements, the Beetle was ready for America. The question remained was, how to get there?

The curious looking Beetle was not a complete stranger to the American public. A few had been brought back into the country by American GI's, many of them car enthusiasts who had become enamored with the little car while stationed overseas. But, as mentioned, the era of big tin was just beginning, as was the whole new sport of "hot rodding," which the Beetle was not exactly suited for.

As for sales in Britain, although they eventually became Volkswagen's fourth largest market, they were slow at first to embrace the Volkswagen. After all, they had just finished a six-year war with the country, and buying most German products was understandably considered taboo. In America, at first, it was the same.

Ben Pon and His Two Beetles

Ben Pon, a Dutch importer/exporter of VW cars, arrived on a ship in New York on January 17, 1949, with two Beetles with the idea of exporting them to America from Holland and establishing a dealer network there. But the venture was nearly doomed before he unloaded the cars. He held a press conference on the ship, the Westerdam, but the journalists who bothered to show up were not impressed. Some were calling it "Hitler's car," despite Pon's continual references to the Beetle as the "Victory Wagon."

Undeterred, Pon shopped the Beetles up and down the east coast to various car dealers, hoping to strike a deal to export the cars, but no one seem interested, to say the least. The Beetle looked downright spartan and tiny compared to the road monsters currently cruising America's highways. Thrifty, modest, compact and economical were not words found in any automotive sales lexicon at the time, so dealers never gave the Beetle much of a chance. Pon finally gave up after three weeks. He sold one of his cars and all of the parts for $800 (to pay his bill at the Roosevelt Hotel) and returned home to Rotterdam empty-handed.

Nordhoff Opens the Door

Later that same year, (1949) he traveled to America himself to sell the little car. Instead of bringing an actual car, he brought pictures and drawings. Upon presenting them in customs, the officer in charge laughed, "No one in the world would buy a car that looked like that."

Americans had just come home from war and they wanted their cars to be bigger, more powerful and flashy. They wanted wide bodies and big fenders. After years of poverty, rationing, and conservation, it was time to let loose, and the Beetle just didn't fit the image. To Nordhoff's dismay, many of the auto dealers he encountered felt the same way, all except for one. Max Hoffman was a New York importer of relatively exotic European sports and luxury cars, but something about the Beetle caught his eye, and he decided to give the little VW a shot.

This now immortal photograph of arguably the first Volkswagen to be officially imported into America. Ben Pon (left) brought two Beetles to the United States in 1949 in an attempt to export them from his native Holland, but he was rebuffed by every dealer he met. He sold off one car after just three weeks, used the money to pay his hotel bill, and returned to Rotterdam without a distribution deal.

Nordhoff gave him the exclusive rights to sell the Beetle in all states east of the Mississippi river.

Slowly, very slowly, the Volkswagen Beetle began to appear on American roads, drawing many curious stares. In 1950, Hoffman imported 157 cars; 390 in 1951; 601 in 1952 and 980 in 1953. At the time, a Standard Beetle sold for $1200 and a Deluxe was sold for $1400, while a sunroof model added $150. The rarely seen convertible would fetch a whopping $1997.

The sales figures were nearly insignificant compared to just about any other country, but then again, Hoffman didn't exactly promote the Beetle either. He felt the little cars wouldn't make much of an impact or catch on, so he chose not to waste much time and money marketing the Beetles. But he was wrong. At the first U.S. International Trade Fair in Chicago in 1951, 20 Beetles were shown, and they got quite a bit of attention.

The following week, the Hoffman Motor Car Co. received orders for 250 cars.

Nordhoff was rather upset by Hoffman's lack of promotion, so he cancelled his deal at the end of 1953 and established two VW sites on each coast: one in New York, the other in San Francisco. With a dedicated staff and corporate backing, the VW reps approached car dealers who seemed to be catering to a younger, hipper audience. More dealers signed on, and the VW numbers quickly began to take off, with sales of 6343 in 1954 and soaring to 35,851 in 1955. In the space of just four years, the U.S. had become VW's largest market outside of Germany.

Behind the Scenes of an Early Beetle Assembly Line

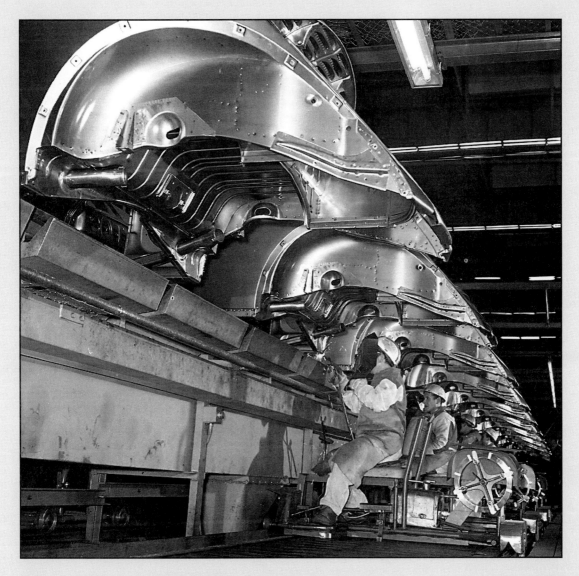

Much of the Beetle's assembly was done by hand. This demonstrates just a few of the thousands of tack welds needed to put a Beetle together. Here a worker adds a few more welds to the rear part of the chassis.

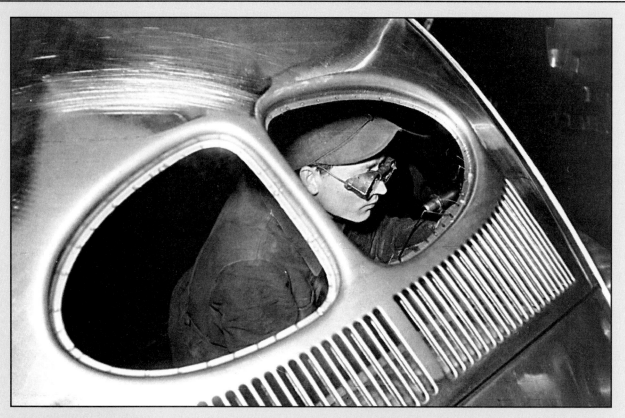

No detail is overlooked. An interesting fact to note is that the main reason for the Split Window is not to add structural rigidity; it is because it was cheaper to produce two smaller windows than one big one.

More welding ensures a stable, rattle-free ride for these Splits. On March 10, 1953, the last Split Window left the factory as an attempt to further distance the car from its pre-war roots. In addition to a number of changes, the main alteration was the presence of a full oval window in the rear. Customers could even buy kits to update their Split Window Beetle to an Oval model.

Out of context, these Split-Window sunroof clips look quite abstract stacked on dollies to be transported to the line. Though the Beetles look to be all one piece, the body actually consists of five major pieces, with the roof and rear window subsection as the largest.

A machine helps tack weld the front quarter panel and roof clip to the rest of the body.

Door frames are meticulously welded in place as the Beetle nears completion.

6

The Beetle Comes to America

The Wallenius Lines, the shipping company contracted to carry Volkswagens across the Atlantic, brought them to docks on the East Coast, and Colley Motorships Ltd. would then transport VWs into the Great Lakes region.

Of the roughly 50,000 cars imported into the United States in 1954, approximately 34,000 were Volkswagens. The little car was rapidly becoming popular, so much so that there were soon waiting lists. The number of dealers at this point was so limited, that "bootleg" Beetles were imported unofficially by gray market dealers. These gray market Beetles accounted for nearly 20 percent of all Beetle sales that year.

The Beetles were not popular with everyone, however. By the mid-'50s, Americans were demanding bigger, and flashier cars more than ever before, and the hot rod and cruising craze was in full swing. Plus, adults

still associated the Beetle with Nazi Germany, which was still fresh in the minds of many. Anti-German sentiment kept many of them from even considering buying a VW. Of course, there was also the issue of practicality. Many families could only afford one car, and with kids, etc., a tiny Beetle was hardly a wise choice when you could have a massive Chevy Nomad.

So, who then, bought the Beetle? Because the Beetle was so much different than anything else in America at the time, it appealed to the mind-set of those who wanted to be different, antiestablishment types who just didn't want to conform to the standard. This

Built in 1959, *Madame Butterfly* could carry 1050 cars to America. She was the largest ship of her kind by the late 1950s.

included students, and those who were the forerunners of the forthcoming "Beat Generation." These people also may have been much younger during the war, and felt the impact much less.

But slowly, the customer base began to become more diversified. As the car became more familiar on the streets, it became more American, less German, in a way, and the Beetle was just another little car to choose from. Even today, most people don't know the Mitsubishi car they're driving or the television they're watching came from the same company that produced the dreaded Zero, or that the technology of the BMW in the driveway came from German airplanes in World War II. People soon learned to buy a product, not a past.

As the Volkswagen carved out its own part of American society, it began to appeal to many on several different levels. First, young people saw it as a cheap and reliable car. Do-it-yourselfers believed that they could work on the simple engine if it ever broke down. The welloff saw it as an ideal inexpensive car for their kids, who were among the Beetle's biggest fans. All of these people followed the Volkswagen philosophy of cars: Think Small. In a news conference in 1954, Heinrich Nordhoff commented on the "bigness" of the American car trends. "The future of the automobile lies in the small car," he stated. "[The large cars] have 10 times more power than can be put to any use and thus violates every principle of engineering and technical science."

Simply put, the Beetle then, as in the coming decades, became trendy to own, and that is the secret behind its success and enduring popularity.

It is interesting to look at the climate of American car buyers in the late '40s and early '50s to help determine why the Volkswagen became so popular in the next decade. Volkswagen, at the time, was leading the way in the small car trend. The number of families with two cars in their garages increased from 4.8 percent in 1948 to 13.8 percent in 1955. However, there was a sur-

Nordhoff stands over the cars produced in a single day in 1955. He was a brilliant strategist, with a clear plan on how to penetrate the American market.

prisingly large share of the American public who owned no car at all, and those people lived mostly in a big city where a big car was simply unpractical and out of the question. Certainly, these people were great candidates for a Beetle.

VW 's Formula for Success

During this time, most car dealers sold a wide variety of brands, not just Volkswagen. Though there were some VW-exclusive dealers, Volkswagen was encouraging even more dealers to "go exclusive" to help bolster U.S. sales. Typical of the German drive much of the world had witnessed only a decade before, Volkswagen, in early 1954, went from sixth to first place in import sales

in the United States, and its sales figures nearly doubled that of its nearest competitor, MG.

In April 1955, Volkswagen America was formed in New York state, though six months later the name was changed to Volkswagen of America. Its main function was to be the distribution arm and operations center for Volkswagenwerks in America. As such, its official function was to coordinate the distribution, sales, importation and service of the Beetle and the Bus.

During the '50s, Volkswagen worked with many different companies in Germany and abroad to develop and construct a wide variety of Beetle-based cars, from Meisen which built ambulances to Hebmüller who built

279,986 total Beetles were produced for the 1955 model year, including the one millionth Beetle on August 5. 81,979 were shipped to the U.S. Prices were dropped.

doorless police cars. One of Nordhoff's strategies was to direct Volkswagen into a stage where it would not divert resources toward off-shoot projects and hence distract from the main focus of building quality small cars. Concentrating all of its efforts on the Beetle, Volkswagen was able to control costs, become more efficient and focus on the push toward success. Of course, exceptions to Nordhoff's rule was the Type II and the Karmann-Ghia coupe and convertible. Stopping most of the supplying of chassis to independent coachbuilders, Nordhoff remarked: "This is a car factory, not a chassis factory. We wish to retain control over the appearance of cars that carry the company name. Simply supplying chassis alone is of no interest to us whatsoever."

Nordhoff's strategy of concentrating on the existing Beetle rather than on developing new models was also part of the Beetle success. He was able to continually direct company resources to refining and improving the Beetle, rather than be distracted by research, development and testing of new cars, which was very costly and time-con-

suming. Instead of concentrating efforts on the development of new models or other brands, engineers were forced to work on improving the Beetle, and each year, many hundreds of improvements, most of which went unnoticed by the general buying public, were added to the Beetle. To the novice, the Beetle seemed never to appear different, never to change, as most all of the improvements happened under the skin.

When the final Beetle rolls off the production line in Mexico some time in the future, the design will have changed so slightly that no one could possibly mistake it for anything but the same Beetle of Nordhoff's day. The shape, the sound and even the smell is the same in our day as it was in Porsche's day. Yet, according to some engineers and auto analysts, the only two things left unchanged between these two Beetles is a clamping strip that holds down the hood and deck lid rubber seals. The rest has been redesigned, changed, altered and designed again, so that parts from a 1949 Beetle would not fit on a 2001 Beetle and vice versa. (We are talking about the Beetles still produced in Mexico, which are true to the original; not the Bugs sold in dealerships today).

The overall success of the company in the '50s through to the '60s and '70s can be attributed to Nordhoff's strategy. Most car companies, when they announced the production of one model, were already designing its replacement. Name one car on the road that was designed in 1936, began mass production in 1946 and is still being made. Only the Beetle has such a long track record.

VW Streamlines Production

Another reason for VW's success is Nordhoff's efforts to continually improve the production line at the factory. When he assumed control, employees needed approximately 400 hours per Volkswagen, causing Nordhoff to exclaim, "If we go on like this, we won't be going on much longer." Getting a car built in 100 hours was one of his primary goals. Though the factory workers were doubtful of the possibility, by 1955 it had been achieved. This improvement in efficiency allowed for a price cut that year. In fact, the Volkswagenwerks was a model of efficiency, the poster child for Germany's post-war economic boom. In 1955, the year of VW's millionth Beetle, 6000 people were added to the factory's payroll, Volkswagen had 970 dealerships in Germany and 2498 in other countries and it accounted for almost half of all German car exports. That year, Volkswagen built a total of 81,979 cars for the U. S. market.

Bye, Bye Split, Hello Oval

Although Nordhoff resisted change, he was open for improvement, and by 1958 it was clear to him that one small design change would definitely help with sales. For years, he had been getting customer complaints about how hard it was to see out of the rear window, which was often cited as major reason why people chose not to buy one. This change was an easy one for VW: Simply increase the size of the window—in fact, why not increase the size of all of the windows? Hence, the Oval Window model was born.

At the same time, they made several other changes in response to customer feedback that made the VW more enjoyable to drive: they removed the uncomfortable roller-ball gas pedal and the turn signals were moved to the top of the fenders.

Why Buy?

The Volkswagen wasn't alone in changing the perception of the value of a smaller, lighter, more economical car. Fiat, Ford, Renault and Opel were also unveiling small cars in response to the Beetle. By 1957, there were over two dozen cars to choose from under $2000.

Beetles were shipped overseas as fast as the company could make them. Here is a 1956 Beetle tied down for its shipment from the factory.

To make each run across the Atlantic as profitable as possible, the VWs were tightly packed and stacked.

This Beetle is being lowered into the hold of the *Rigoletto*, one of two specialized vessels destined for California.

The port at Rotterdam soon became the main point of departure for VW's bound for America. In 1956, Wallenius Lines signed a contract with VW for five years, with an optional two-year extension. When signed, the agreement was the largest in Swedish shipping history. Here, workers get yet another shipment of Beetles ready for the journey to America.

Row after row of Oval-Window VWs leave the factory and await transport, mostly to America. Note, against popular belief, the whitewall tires were an option offered at the factory as well as the dealership.

The Beetle's Golden Era

7

Perhaps the most illustrious period in Beetle history is the 1960s, when the Beetle would reached the very peak of its popularity, embraced by the Beat generation as the ultimate antiestablishment vehicle. Despite competition from just about every manufacturer, the VW just kept selling and selling in greater numbers.

Many car makers fought back by unleashing a wide range of cars aimed at future Volkswagen buyers. In 1960, 614,000 cars (not necessarily Beetles) were imported into the United States, while, in 1961, that number fell nearly in half to approximately 339,000. Late in the '50s, there were close to two dozen small foreign cars offered in the U.S. market for under $2000. The first Volvos and Saabs began to arrive, as did cars such as Messerschmidts, Isettas, Opel Rekords and DKWs. Simcas and Panhards, Renaults and Dauphines, Citroens and Fiats were also imported to take on VW. Japan was also testing the waters, sending over the first Toyopets and PL210s, from Toyota and Datsun factories, but they couldn't even make a dent in the American market and they quickly disappeared. However the small car appeared to Americans, regardless from what shore it arrived, each foreign import played a small roll in the acceptance of compact cars, and each car company accepted meant money in the bank.

American Manufacturers Fight Back

American car manufacturers, slow to appreciate the nature of a changing market in the '50s, soon realized they had better get into the small car game. The Big Three

launched the Valiant, the Ford Falcon, and Chevy Corvair (the closest clone of a Beetle with a rear-mounted, four-cylinder, air-cooled engine, not to mention an IRS rear suspension system). In 1959, Ford introduced the Anglia at the Earl's Court Motor Show in England. The sales staff on hand were issued brochures on how to sell the car to prospective Beetle buyers. It even went so far as to urge its staff to point out that engineers and journalists had found the Beetle to be "not only crude in design and mediocre in performance, but difficult and even dangerous to drive." Some of the drawbacks in the pamphlet suggested the show staff point out the VW's noisy third gear (the gear that most drivers spend the most time in), that it is prone to oversteer, that it lacks adequate luggage space and the heater could blow fumes into the cabin. Of course, Volkswagen recognized these shortcomings and offered many changes in the future to correct them.

Though not able to last for more than a few years in the U.S. market previously, the early '60s became a boom for the small car manufacturer. Of course, the company on top remained Volkswagen. The new model in 1958 helped Volkswagen sell cars well into the next decade. The new Oval Window was a vast improvement, and women loved the new gas pedal—high heels didn't work well with the roller style accelerator. The front window was enlarged, making the new Beetle appear lighter, airier and generally more pleasant to drive. Of course a main advantage of the window improvements was that it was safer to drive and easier to navigate. There were also new colors.

As 1959 drew to a close, Beetle sales were

higher than ever. More than 150,000 VWs were imported to the U.S.—officially. Demand was so high, that there were long waiting lists, which fueled the creation of gray market Beetles, so it is not certain how many were really imported total. Estimates put the number of gray market Beetles to be as high as 30,000.

Advertising

Apart from a brief ad campaign in 1958 by the J. M. Mathes agency, Volkswagen of America used little advertising. Instead, they relied on automotive press reviews and word of mouth.

Dr. Carl Hahn

Dr. Carl Hahn, was the head of Volkswagen of America at the time. Hahn had served as Nordhoff's personal assistant as well as the head of export sales and promotion only five years before. He earned his Ph.D. from the University of Bern in Switzerland, and was later promoted to the board of management in Wolfsburg in 1963. As head of VWofA, Hahn had decided that the only way to really be competitive with the Big Three in America was to advertise. As it was, he figured VW could only sell approximately 150,000 Volkswagens each year by the methods they currently employed. To Hahn, this was unacceptable, and, as luck would have it, he decided to make this change literally months before the American car companies were scheduled to unleash a fleet of small cars to compete with VW.

Over the course of several months, Hahn met with scores of advertising teams and literally thousands of ad men. He was disappointed in the same material they all seemed to present him, a conservative approach to advertising, something traditional for the day. As Hahn said, "All we saw were presentations that showed Volkswagen ads that looked exactly like every other ad. The only difference was that where the tube of tooth-

paste had been, they had placed a Volkswagen." In short, overanalyzed results from test boards and impact studies caused the ads to become stale, safe and homogenized. Volkswagen was a different type of car, and Hahn demanded a different kind of advertising.

Hahn turned to Doyle, Dane and Bernbach, a relatively new advertising company that was known for their highly creative, unique approach to advertising. Their client roster was diverse, ranging from the department store chain Ohrbachs to Polaroid. Arthur Stanton was a Volkswagen distributor and a member of the VW ad committee under Hahn, and he especially liked the creativity behind the Ohrbach ads. After hiring them to do a series of ads for his dealership, Queensboro Motors, he suggested them to Hahn and the committee. Instead of offering a presentation on what they thought VW ads should look like, they merely showed the committee some work they had done for other companies. Hahn's group liked what they saw and gave them the account—as well as $800,000 to get started.

The creative end of the company, art director Helmut Krone and copywriter Julian Koenig, hopped a flight to Wolfsburg to witness the effort and skill that it took to build Beetles. There, they met with engineers, executives, and men on the assembly lines. They learned production techniques, quality control and actual test results of the car's performance. They learned how costs could be reduced in service with a standardized parts list, and how the traction of the rear wheels was better accomplished because of the rear-mounted engine.

Back in New York, Krone, Koenig and their teams churned out ad after ad, giving the American public a whole new impression of the Volkswagen, what it was like to buy one, own one, drive one and repair one, and the appearance of the ad never changed. The style of wording didn't either. It was straightforward and factual. Each headline ends with a period, symbolizing, not the end of any sentence, but a statement of fact. "The Volkswagen is $1.02 a pound because it is a frugal car to own, economical and practical.", read one ad. We don't have anything to show you in our new model, because nothing flashy or fancy had changed, only underneath the skin, was Volkswagen's philosophy on building cars.

Honesty was everything. The copy in the ads were facts. There were no rude comments about competitive cars, no direct comparisons or cheap shots. The ads focused on the positive attractions of the Volkswagen and left out the negative aspects of other cars on the markets then. People responded, especially since a lot of ads appeared to make fun of the Volkswagen itself.

By 1960, the VW ad budget topped out at $1.5 million, and, by comparison, other companies were spending five times that to push similarly small cars. . . but the VW beat them all.

Small. Medium. Large.

A long time ago we made our first Volkswagen. It held 4 people comfortably and about 4 pieces of luggage just as comfortably. It could go 27 miles on a gallon of gas. And about 40,000 miles on a set of tires.

We called it the bug.

Then a little later on we made another Volkswagen. It was for families who were too big for the bug. This new Volkswagen had enough room for eight people and thirteen pieces of luggage. (About thirteen more bags than you could fit into most station wagons that hold eight people.)

We called it a box.

And for a while, everybody was happy. Then we began to find out that for a lot of people the box was too much Volkswagen, and the bug not enough.

So we made the Squareback sedan. (In case you haven't noticed, it's the one in the picture between the bug and the box.)

It's a lot bigger inside than the beetle and a lot smaller than the box. (It's got enough room for 4 people and about 5 valises. Or 2 people and about 15 valises.)

Our new Squareback has a 65 h.p. air-cooled engine that averages 27 m.p.g. Which is pretty good for a car that can go 84 m.p.h.

It also has disc brakes, torsion bar suspension and synchromesh transmission. As a matter of fact everything you've come to expect from a VW.

On behalf of everybody here, we'd like to welcome it to the family.

Impossible.

Has the Volkswagen fad died out?

© 1960 VOLKSWAGEN

Think small.

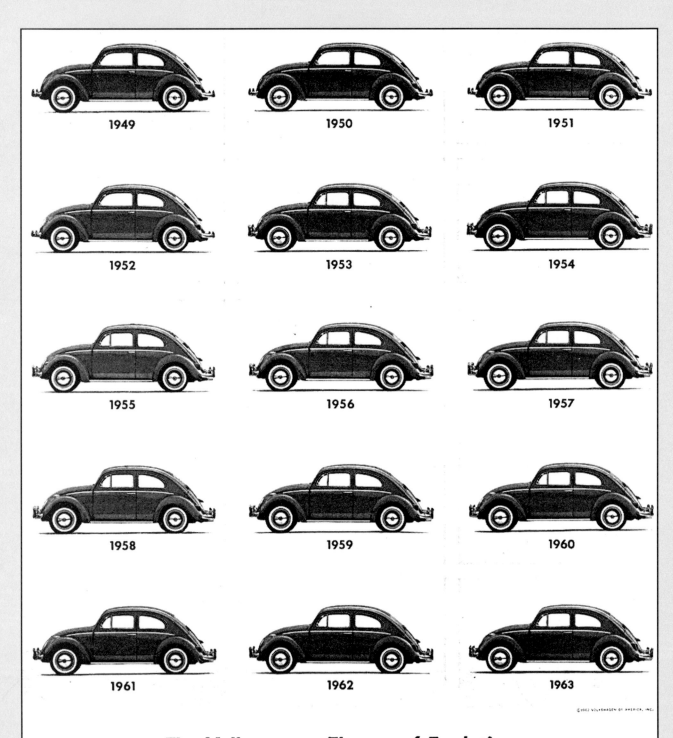

1949 1950 1951 1952 1953 1954 1955 1956 1957 1958 1959 1960 1961 1962 1963

The Volkswagen Theory of Evolution.

Ugly is only skin-deep.

The Beetle
and Latin America

8

For the 1968 model year, the Volkswagen was beginning its evolution toward a safety-regulated car, which would eventually lead to its downfall. Bumper changes and padded dashes are just a few things that helped it meet safety standards in the U.S. Safety issues were not nearly so strict in some Latin American countries around the world, where the Beetle thrived.

What was next? 1967 was a pivotal year for Volkswagen. It had completed the transition into the 12-volt automotive world. The old styling of the original Beetle was still fairly intact, as the '67 Beetle looked nearly the same as a '47 Beetle. Volkswagen had built 1,127,587 Volkswagens and 812,959 of them (over 72 percent) ended up in the United States. With the U.S. market firmly established, VW could concentrate on conquering the rest of the world, which it had begun some years earlier with its partners in Brazil and Mexico, which would both prove pivotal to keeping the VW alive long after it was no longer exported to the U.S.

Volkswagen in Brazil

The love affair between Brazil and the Beetle or Fusca, as it is known there, began with a Brazilian importer for Chrysler, Jose Bastos Thompson, who realized that large American cars weren't practical for Brazil's narrow streets, poor roads and struggling economy. What the country's people needed, not unlike pre-war Germany people, was a "people's car." They needed a car that was easy to manufacture, simple to repair, reliable and rugged enough to traverse the country's poorly maintained roads.

When Nordhoff visited Brazi in the interest of setting up a factory, Thompson further convinced him that building a factory in Brazil would greatly benefit VW. It would reduce Wolfsburg's shipping costs and bolster Brazil's economy. With 80 percent of the funding from Germany, Volkswagen de

Brasilia was founded in March 1953 and soon began assembling Beetles from pre-fabricated kits shipped over from Germany. Three years later, it employed 200 workers and had assembled over 2800 cars. Later that year, a large production factory was built and by 1957 the first Brazilian-built Volkswagen, a Transporter, rolled off the line. By 1959 they were building Beetles entirely from the ground up.

Brazilian Beetles were different than German-made Beetles. They had lower compression engines and stiffer suspension. The Brazilian factory still uses the pre-1965 body style (with the wide A- and C-pillars), but adds to it the upright headlights attached to later-style fenders. In only three years, the Beetle became the best-selling car in the country, and 10 years after that, 1972, the 1,000,000th Brazilian Beetle was built.

They not only built Type Is and IIs, but branched out and constructed many cars that were not seen in other parts of the world, including a four-door Type III, the popular Brasilia and the sleek SP2 (which they planned to export until it was discovered that the headlights were positioned too low to meet the standards of most exporting countries). After following most of the changes made to the Beetle in Germany, the early '80s models were given smaller engines, the 1300, to reduce fuel consumption until a year later the 1600 was proven to provide more efficient combustion.

When VW introduced their watercooled models, it wasn't long before the limited production space had to be prioritized. In 1986, after building 3.3 million Beetles, the Brazilian assembly line stopped producing the Beetle, but it would prove to be temporary. It was resurrected in 1993 by the renamed Volkswagen de Brasilia, Autolatina. As before, the Beetle was well-suited for the narrow, rough roads in the jungle. Although it sold well, production was very limited, with only 33,000 units sold through the mid-'90s. This version of the Beetle was modified

Volkswagen's 1968 product line. Clockwise from lower left: Sunroof Beetle, Transporter, Fastback, Karmann-Ghia and Squareback.

in the mid-'90s to meet Brazil's crash-test standards. The 1584cc engine is fitted with dual carburetors instead of fuel injection, and an optional alcohol-burning version was available. It is cobbled with a three-way catalytic converter, but did have electronic injection, safety glass and front disc brakes, all very modern technology by Brazilian automotive standards.

Volkswagen in Mexico

Though not in production as long as the Brazilian Beetle, the Mexican Beetle has become much more popular. Like Brazil, VW Mexico began assembling VW kits in 1954. But Volkswagen de Mexico would not be established for another 10 years, and it would still take three more years, until 1967, before the first VW rolled off the assembly line at the Pueblo plant, approximately 80 miles from Mexico City.

Mexico went wild over the Beetle, but

In 1974, the last Beetle rolled off the assembly line in Germany to make way for the Passat and other water-cooled cars. Beetles were still being made in other parts of the world, however, mainly in Mexico.

poverty kept many from owning one. By 1975, one-half million Beetles had been built, with a daily output of 550 cars. When production ended in Wolfsburg and Emden, Germany, Mexico became the only plant in the world where Beetles were still being produced. They even exported some back to Europe, though demand was small.

The cars were based on the pre-1971 body style and were given the 1200cc engine, but added features included the fuel gauge, rear defroster, inertia seatbelts and adjustable headrests. Some even had the Wolfsburg crest on the horn button. Mexico built the 20 millionth Beetle on May 15, 1981, and as a result, produced 2400 special edition Silver Bugs to commemorate the occasion. Because these were so popular, Mexico initiated a series of special editions. As the world's only supplier of VWs, Mexico was busy shipping them to all parts of the world.

However, as time went on, new legislation restricted the sales of VWs in many countries. Retooling to adjust the cars to these new laws was very expensive, and sales could not support the changes. The last Mexican Beetles to enter Europe were sold in Germany in 1985. So VW de Mexico began to concentrate on producing VWs solely for its own market. But rather than move forward with technology, the cars seem to take a step or two back. The fresh air ventilation was removed, as were the rear heater outlets and rear seatbelts. The dual-circuit brakes were scrapped in 1985 (but reinstated in 1990). They finally added a catalytic converter in 1991.

The 21 millionth Beetle was built on June 23, 1992, and 6000 21 Millones Special Edition Beetles were produced (actually, they were sold before they were even built). In 1994, the flat-four engine was changed for the first time in Mexico, with the addition of fuel injection, hydraulic lifters and an oil filter. The next year, the generator was replaced by an alternator and front disc brakes became standard. In 1996, most of the chrome was gone, and an economic slump halted production during the summer of that year. It never fully recovered, and numbers decreased from 450 cars per day to barely 100. The Beetle is wildly popular in Mexico City, where most of the taxicabs are all green and white Beetles. The legacy lives on.

The Mexican plant kept the VW Beetle alive with special models like this 1975 LeGrande Bug.

Other Beetle-Based Models

9

The Volkswagen Transporter became a popular vehicle to carry many people and/or cargo. These two were owned by the Hotel Packard in Havana, Cuba. Photo courtesy James Brooks.

The Beetle's success ultimately led to the creation of several models that were Beetles in spirit, if not in body. That is to say, the models may have had different body styles and appearances, but the underpinnings and the design theme were related to or inspired by the Beetle, and the influence is unmistakable. As the Beetle began to rise in popularity, Nordhoff and his staff began to introduce other models to ride the Beetle's wave of success. Here's a look at some of the more interesting models.

Type II

Although it may seem ridiculous that the boxy, van-like Transporter is based on the Beetle, one look at the bug-eyed front fascia and it is clear to see the relationship. Look further under the skin, and you'll see the platform, suspension, rear-engine and drive-train are but slightly modified versions of the Beetle.

Although officially dubbed the Transporter, VW owners called them van or bus. The bus became exceptionally popular with protesting students and hippies of the '60s, many of them calling it home as they traveled throughout the U.S., attending protests and rock concerts.

The Transporter's Roots

Ben Pon was most famous for his first failed attempt to export the Beetle to the U.S., he is also credited with coming up with the basic idea and design of the Transporter, a little known fact. The idea of a vehicle

The Single Cab (seen on the right) was added to the Type II family in September 1952. It was an excellent idea, considering the post-war building boom and the up-swing of the economy.

Like the Beetles before it, the Type II received the same tightly packed treatment for its voyage across the Atlantic.

with increased passenger capacity was nothing new around the factory. In fact, it was part of Porsche's original plan to offer a truck or van in addition to the Beetle. After the war, Ivan Hirst directed the VW designers to build a commercial flatbed truck based on the Beetle platform, called the Plattenwagen. These were used as parts haulers around the VW factory, and were so reliable that the last one was finally retired in 1994. But Hirst wasn't thinking about consumers, only commercially. Pon saw the Plattenwagens and was convinced that something similar would work with con-

This Panel Bus was delivered to the dealership without the hubcaps and windshield wipers.

sumers in his native Holland. In 1947, he tried to get the Plattenwagen (now fitted with body panels) certified as a street-legal vehicle in his home country. When rejected, he sketched the Transporter in a notebook. It would not only be something that could be used to transport goods to and from businesses, but to haul people as well.

VW development chief Alfred Haesner hired additional men and material to work on the project in the fall of 1948. At first called the Type 29, the Transporter sketches were in two forms, one with a straight, flat driver's cab and the other with a slightly angled, swept front end with a projecting roofline. Heinrich Nordhoff saw them for the first time on November 20, 1948, and he chose the second version. After some testing of various components, the first completed car was ready by March 11 the following year with testing to begin that April. It was determined that the original Beetle chassis was not strong enough to handle the additional load. The plans were redrawn and additional prototypes constructed.

In 1949, eight Type IIs, as they were called, were built and went on display with production to begin as early as 1950. By the same time next year, a handful of the new vehicles had made their way to the United States, but they weren't officially imported until 1952 (and only 10 were sold that year). They were offered at roughly $2000 which was about $600 more than the Sedan, but it was well within the market price for a similar vehicle.

The Type II Expands

Soon after its introduction, the Type II developed a rather devout following, and Nordhoff ordered that the brand be expanded with different models. The DeLuxe carried up to eight passengers and was priced about $200 higher than the standard model, which had been reduced to $1995 in 1952.

Two years later, there were six models to choose from: 1) Eight-passenger Microbus (note: early VW promotional literature referred to the passenger vehicles as "Micro Buses," but the single word, Microbus was soon adopted instead. A Golde sunroof was offered as an option. 2) The DeLuxe Microbus was equipped with a Golde sunroof, windows in the rear corners and eight observation windows in the roof. This is now referred to as a 23-Window Bus or a Samba, perhaps the most sought-after of all the Type IIs. 3) The Kombi was a slightly knocked-down version of the Microbus. The seats were removable to allow for passengers or cargo (hence Kombi refers to combination, either a passenger van, a cargo van or a combination of the two), the rear side windows opened toward the rear for extra ventilation and the cargo area lacked a complete interior and/or headliner. 4) A Delivery Van or Panel Bus was offered as a strictly commercial vehicle. It featured no windows and very little in the way of an interior. 5) The Pickup Truck featured a flat bed with side and rear gates that lowered. Notable was the "treasure chest," a large compartment underneath the bed that offered additional locking cargo holding area. 6) Finally, the ambulance and fire truck versions were offered.

The basic construction of the Type II was unitized, meaning that the body was one complete piece with no attached panels. This was supported by a ladder frame attached to the floor pan. The front axle was modified from the Beetle's so that the top torsion bar was four-leaf and the bottom three-leaf, while the swing-arm rear end was the same as the Beetle except for the reduction gears (similar to that of the Kübelwagen during wartime). Braking was accomplished through 230mm drums on all corners.

On November 12, 1949, the Type II was introduced to the press, and the designers called it, "a combination of a unitized body with the main characteristics of a Volkswagen." Production officially began in March 1950 with 10 produced each day. By the end of the year, production had increased to 60 units a day. Four years later, close to 100,000 Type IIs were in service around the world.

In the mid-'50s, Volkswagen specifically suggested five main benefits to owning a Bus: 1) They could haul more cargo, almost 170 cubic feet, or two-thirds of the total interior space. 2) With the loading door on the side of the vehicle instead of at the rear, the driver didn't have to leave the sidewalk or stand in the gutter to load his cargo. As well, the doors were wide and the floor lower than most, both for loading and unloading heavy and bulky items. 3) With no wasted space, design or weight, there was nothing "extra" stealing potential cargo-hauling power from the economical engine. 4) The weight distribution offered a smooth ride, with the help of the suspension. 5) The engine enjoyed a low fuel consumption, roughly 24mph, fully loaded.

In addition to these, it is important to note that no other transporter in its class offered roof-mounted ventilation, such weight distribution (with the driver in front and the engine in the rear) as well as an unobstructed view of the road in any direction.

In 1966, production of the Type II had increased to 750 units a day from the Hanover plant, and Volkswagen commanded nearly 80 percent of the market. Its nearest competitor was the Ford Transit and the Hanomag F20, which only produced 220 and 55 units a day, respectively.

The following year (for the 1968 model year), the Bus got a facelift. Under the supervision of design chief Gustav Mayer, planning for a new Type II had begun way back in 1964. Many changes improved the stiffness of the body/frame, increased the interior space (thanks to the use of double joint rear axle with semi-trailing links). The engine was now the 1600cc borrowed from the Type III, and the transmission was from the Beetle, only with a modified fourth-gear ratio. Most notably was the one-piece front window, which is now commonly referred to as a "bay window."

The lineup of models didn't change much, with the exception of the renaming of the

By the time the Type III reached America, there were three to choose from. Though they looked very similar from the front, they got their names based on the rear ends. From left to right (bottom photo): The Notchback, the Fastback and the Squareback.

DeLuxe 23-Window. Instead of Samba, it was referred to as the Clipper L, which soon sparked a lawsuit against Volkswagen in America, because Pan Am had already copyrighted that name for use in their airline. The name was soon dropped.

Type III

As the Beetle was gaining market share in the U.S. board members at VW were considering if they should either replace or at least remodel the Beetle. If not replace it, then perhaps make another version to complement and expand the line. The board was

divided on what to do, however. Heinrich Nordhoff, let it "slip" at the 1960 Geneva Car Salon, that Volkswagen was making plans for a new car, a bigger, better Volkswagen. Details about the car were partially released in the U.S. by VW's press agency, UPI, in March of that year, and magazines were given pre-production test drives later that year. The official unveiling of the VW 1500 didn't come until the Frankfurt International Auto Show in September 1961, more than a year later.

At first, most people called the VW 1500, as it was officially known, a Beetle in dis-

From 1969 on (for the 1970 model year), the Type IIIs had reinforced bumpers much like the Beetles as well as some other exterior changes.

The pancake engine, as it was nicknamed, used in all Type IIIs, was basically that of the Beetle's engine with the exception of the relocated fan.

guise. The Type III sedan, now referred to as a Notchback due to its apparent cut-out rear end, had a squared look but it was six inches longer and three inches wider than the Beetle, though it utilized its pan and similar wheel base. There was more room for the passengers in the 1500 because it didn't narrow down toward the front like the Beetle did. The engine was still in the rear, under a cargo area and the VW 1500 boasted two

With a dramatic increase in cargo carrying ability, the Squareback could be ordered like this, for passenger use, or without rear windows in delivery van trim.

storage areas, one in the rear and the other under the uniquely squared hood, designed to better fit the European cars of the day. The idea behind its design was to give buyers the ability to "trade up" to a better model, with a larger engine, more room and better performance. Albeit, the price increased to where it was $300 more than the Beetle 1200.

Most of the design elements of the Beetle chassis also were used in the VW 1500, with the exception of the torsion bars and the sub-assembly that held the transmission, axles and engine. The torsion bars were twice as long as the Beetle's and they stretched from one side of the vehicle to the other and were jointed, allowing for a softer ride. To help combat engine noise and vibration, the rear swing-arm axle, though typically Beetle in concept, was connected via a subframe and insulated with rubber dampers between it and the chassis. The steering was improved to utilize cam and rollers instead of the worm and nut steering of the Beetle.

On the dashboard (the upper part was padded), three round pods contained the instruments, the 150km/h speedometer in the middle, the clock to the right and the fuel gauge to the left that also held the directional lights, parking lights, high beams, generator and oil pressure warning lights. On the left of the three pods was the switch panel containing four ivory-colored knobs that controlled the wipers, washer, parking lights and headlights.

For 1964, in Europe, Volkswagen offered the S (which aptly stood for "Sport") models for its VW 1500 lineup (Notch- and Squareback). They still used the same engine, but it was dual carbureted instead and the output was increased to 66hp. With the addition of chrome trim throughout the car, the interior was re-trimmed with new seats and a new 160km/h speedometer. The base model was renamed the 1500N and the two versions sold simultaneously for the same price. The S model didn't have a strong following, especially considering that most people were disappointed to discover that what they were buying was definitely not a sports car. Two years later, the S was replaced by yet another model, the VW 1600TL, which stood for Tourenlimousine, or touring sedan. That same year, the VW 1500N became the VW 1500A, and then it is replaced by the 1600A (and at the same time, the L model was produced). The only difference between the 1600A and the 1600TL was that it had a single carburetor while the TL was dual carbureted.

Of course, despite these improvements, not everyone was glad to see the new cars. Some found them a disappointment, while others decided they were unreliable and unattractive. One thing was for sure, they definitely weren't the Beetle they were used to.

Squareback

The Squareback finally arrived in the U.S. in 1965 for the 1966 model year. Though production of the car, billed as the Wagon or Variant in Europe, had gone on since its debut in February 1962, it was slow in arriving. Since the early '50s, Opel was crowned the leader in station wagon sales in Europe, commanding nearly 45 percent of the market. With this in mind, Volkswagen introduced their Wagon to muscle in on some of Opel's business. Identical to the Sedan (at least until the B pillar), the Squareback featured a station wagon appearance, obviously, but the main differences were in the interior. The rear seat could be folded down flat to allow for additional cargo space. The rear hatch was large, as wide as the back of the car, and the slits for intake, heating and ventilation were in the rear fenders. Two versions were offered, both identical, but one could carry 375kgs. while the other 460kgs because of an additional torsion bar in the rear.

Fastback

Arguably the most unsuccessful VW model to date was the VW1600TL, otherwise known as the Fastback. Production began in 1965. The new sloping roofline made the car sensitive to side winds, offered poor rearward visibility and was rear heavy when filled with a reasonable amount of cargo. Some advantages were found in the engine (85.5mm bore and 69mm stroke), as

the lower compression ratio (7.7:1) gave it more low end torque (11.2mkg) at 2000rmp compared to the 1500S's 10.8mkg at 2200rmps. This meant that it could handle better in city traffic, and it even had better fuel economy. Even though it never sold well, the Fastback was a model that became a mainstay in the lineup until it was discontinued in 1973.

Karmann-Ghia

Even if it appeared that Nordhoff commanded a one-car-model rule (besides the Bus, of course) in the 1950s, one car decidedly made the exception, the Karmann-Ghia. After the successful introduction of the Karmann Beetle Cabriolet, the Wilhelm Karmann GmbH company, the designer, suggested that a more elegant and sporty model of Volkswagen be introduced. The first meeting between Dr. Wilhelm Karmann Jr. (son of the company founder) and Ludwig Boehner, head of VW development in early 1950, ended without results. Several times later, Karmann approached Nordhoff with this idea and each time was refused. Nordhoff was more interested in developing and refining the Beetle and felt that the war-torn German economy wasn't ready for an expensive sports car. However, three years later, Karmann discussed the idea of a Beetle-based sports car with Luigi Serge, the commercial director of the Italian design studio Carrozzeria Ghia. Karmann wanted Carrozzeria Ghia to build a prototype sports car that might convince Nordhoff to change his mind. Karmann was well known for his convertible designs, so he suggested that they go topless. From this meeting with Serge, nothing was finalized and no plans were made. The project was kept secret from Nordhoff, and in fact, Karmann never saw the car either until it was finished. To his pleasant surprise, the car was a coupe, not a convertible.

On November 16, 1953, Heinz Nordhoff saw the prototype sports car for the first

A four-seat convertible version of the 1500 was built by Karmann and introduced at the Frankfurt Auto Show in 1961 but never made it into production.

Though it was Volkswagen's sportiest car, the Karmann-Ghia was known to many as the world's slowest sports car.

time, and was surprisingly pleased given his earlier position. Perhaps it was the elegant flowing lines of the vehicle or the sleek pillar-less doors and curved windows. His only reservation was that he felt it was too costly to produce. But Karmann offered a deal whereby his company would take delivery of rolling chassis Beetles, produce the sports car bodies, assemble the new vehicles and deliver them to the Volkswagen dealers to be sold to the public.

When Nordhoff first approved the plan to partner with Karmann and build the new car, it didn't even have a name. Dr. Wilhelm Karmann, Jr. came up with the name Karmann-Ghia (early sales literature didn't hyphenate the name, but over time, it became popular to do so) to give equal credit to the design studio as well as the coach builder.

However, it wasn't as simple to produce as they thought. First, the Beetle chassis had to be widened by 80mm. The steering wheel needed to be angled downward and the gear lever shortened to match the lowered seating position. Other than that, it was all Beetle under the flashy body, even down to the 36hp engine and transmission in the rear and the suspension and brakes at the four corners. Drawing on all of the skills of the

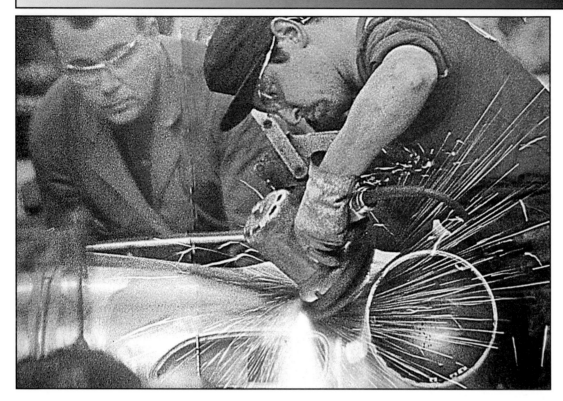

Each car was virtually hand-made, as each seamless body had to be welded together from several different panels.

Italian studio's craftsmen, the curvaceous body required over a dozen pieces of metal to be shaped and welded together for the seamless body. The curve in the fender had to be made in two sections and welded together, and it took approximately 185 workers to make a complete body.

The official launch of the Karmann-Ghia was scheduled for August 1955 but had to be moved forward only because Karmann's small factory didn't have the space to store that many cars. Instead, it was introduced to the public July 14, 1955, but models weren't available to the U.S. until 1956, selling for $2395. Though many were captivated with its looks, it soon became apparent that the performance was not up to par. The 1200cc engine might have been fine for an inexpensive Beetle Sedan, but a sleek sports car deserved a beefier powerplant. The design seemed to promise more than it delivered. Nevertheless, not everyone was so concerned about speed, and there were plenty of buyers who snapped them up as quickly as they arrived in the U.S. Even though they were roughly 75 percent more expensive than a Beetle, sales soared and production

numbers reached 283,501 Karmann-Ghia coupes and 80,897 convertibles (with an additional 23,577 coupes made in Brazil).

The Karmann-Ghia received all of the updates the Beetle did with the exception of the MacPhearson struts in 1970, which wouldn't fit under the front fenders. In late 1957, the ragtop version debuted at the Frankfurt Auto Show. It was heavier because of the stiffened body and hence slower because it employed the same engine. True to convertibles, it cost about 25 percent more than the coupe.

Except for the mandated larger taillights and heavier bumpers (with a wraparound style added later), the Karmann-Ghia changed very little over its lifetime, which ended in June of 1974 to make way for Volkswagen's new Scirocco.

The Super Beetle

Car safety was on the mind of every American legislator during the late 1960s, and every year newer, more stringent regulations were enacted. The Beetle did not adapt very well to these changes, especially in appearance. The simple, round, harmo-

The eight-page brochure for the Karmann-Ghia showed the potential buyer a sportier side of Volkswagen and had a two-page fold-out for the convertible model. Once behind the wheel, they weren't fooled, but sales steadily increased during its production run.

nious shape did not take well to larger bumpers, upright headlights and raised bumper height (causing the hood and deck lid to shorten slightly). All of these regulations, as well as increasing market competition, led VW to develop the Super Beetle, an attempt to modernize the Beetle that ultimately failed. The first model appeared in 1971.

Four versions were eventually available: the 1302, 1302S, 1303 and the 1303S. The appearance of the Super Beetle was quite different from the original models and the changes went farther than skin deep. Both engine choices, the 1300 and the 1600 became dual port for improved breathing. Though the engines of the Super Beetle and the standard model were relatively the same 60-hp unit (only with three extra horses squeezed out of them), the Super's weight characteristics (an additional 155 pounds) caused its power to diminish considerably as compared to the old model. Accelerating a Super to 60mph took approximately 18 seconds and the quarter mile was finished in an unimpressive 21 seconds with a top speed of 64mph. In other words, the Super Beetle wasn't all that Super.

1302 and 1302S Super Beetles

For the 1971 and '72 model years, the Super Beetle stood by its 1200 and 1300 cousins (while the 1500 was dropped) as the "new" Beetle. The front suspension now lacked the torsion bars the car had been equipped with for the last 30 years, and instead rode on MacPherson struts. The car was longer, wider and taller. It weighed more and cost more. Inside, the trunk was redesigned and space almost doubled. This was possible due to the MacPherson struts, which created enough room over the torsion bars to lay the spare tire down flat. The trunk lid was also enlarged and the gas tank pushed back.

From behind, the Super looked the same as the 1970 model, but from the front, there was no mistake that the new car had gone under the knife. The windshield had a larger curve, and new fenders gave the Super a wider and more powerful stance. The engine was the 1300cc powerplant originally used in the Type III, but had been modified with the upright fan of the old Beetle. Or, buyers

In 1971, Volkswagen introduced what it hoped would be the "new" Beetle, the Super Beetle. That same year, Volkswagen produced and sold a record number of cars. On the road, the 1971 Super Beetle looked stronger, wider and safer, an image Volkswagen tried to cultivate in the mid-'70s, but it was too late.

These Beetles obviously weren't destined for the U.S., as they were equipped with the "elephant feet" taillights of a 1973 and later, but still had the flat windshields of the 1971 and 1972 years.

could opt for the 1600cc, a more powerful version of the 1500cc engine from the late 1960s. Both engines had dual-port heads and a modified lubrication system. The front wheels were fitted with disc brakes for the 1302S, while the 1302 was given this as an option. The 1972 1302 model enjoyed the attention as the year's production of the Beetle overtook that of the Model T on February 17, 1972 and became the most widely built car in the world. It would last two years until Volkswagen again made changes, so much so that they had to rename the car once again.

In an effort to comply with all of the new safety laws enacted in the late '60s and early '70s, Volkswagen began crash-testing their product to ensure the best quality in their equipment and design.

1303 and 1303S Super Beetles: The Beginning of the End

For the 1973 model year, the Volkswagen Beetle received its next and last major changes and with them came the renaming of the Super Beetle to the 1303 and 1303S trim packages. Most obvious changes occurred on the outside with the enlarged front windshield. The panoramic windshield had a large pronounced curve in the glass that added approximately 44 percent more forward viewing, but looked out of proportion with the rest of the car. Of course, changes like this cost VW millions in remanufacturing and redesign. Plus, they now had to adhere to ever-tightening safety measures from its most popular export country, the U.S. The front hood was shortened to allow for the larger window, as well as this was the first year VW didn't have a front badge on the hood. The rear fenders were redesigned to fit the enlarged "elephant feet" taillights, and the bumpers became fortified to resist low-impact crashes. Volkswagen called this car, "the most dramatic styling changes since the familiar Bug first came to America." Most customers were turned off and sales diminished. After a few fleeting attempts at gaining new market interest with special additions, the hardtop Super Beetle was discontinued, and only convertibles were still being produced. Mean-while, to make room for a new line of cars, in 1973 the Type III was killed and so too the Type IV the following year. These models were canceled to make room for a new generation of watercooled VWs, led by the Passat.

It was decided by Rudolf Leiding, then the CEO of VWAG from 1971 to 1975, that the Volkswagen Beetle wasn't going to be replaced. Not only could nothing replace it in the hearts and minds of its loyal followers, but the main reason was the technology used or legislated in all U.S. cars by 1973 could no longer be applied to the Beetle.

In a 1974 article in *Small Wonder*, VW's owner magazine, it stated: "There are no plans to stop production of the Beetle...You don't scrap a winner." Ironically, on July 1, 1974, the last Beetle rolled off the Wolfsburg assembly plant. However, other plants around the world continue to produce them, particularly Mexico.

The last stop for a 1973 Super Beetle. The windshield is drastically rounded and the taillights are now larger.

Several coachbuilders in Europe used the Volkswagen's chassis as a basis for a car. Notable ones include the Hebmüller, the Dannenhauer and Stauss, and this 1955 Beutler, produced in Thun, Switzerland.

The End for U.S. Beetles

In America, the last Beetle Sedans went on sale in 1977, and no more convertible Super Beetles were imported, regardless of the fact that the factory in Emden was still churning out over 1000 Beetles a day. In the U.S., only the convertible remained. Finally, on January 19, 1978, the last Volkswagen to be built in Europe drove out the main door of the Emden plant. For millions of Beetle fans, it was the end of an era. The Volkswagen Beetle was no longer invincible.

PART II:

VW
By the Numbers
Year by Year
Model
Changes

1945

Chassis Numbers: 052000 to 053814
Engine Numbers: 077683 to 079093
Produced between January 1, 1945 and December 31, 1945

By the beginning of 1945, the end of World War II was drawing near, but the factory was still producing military vehicles, mostly because its employees had nothing else to do. By February, production reached roughly 2030 units (most of which were Kübelwagens and sedans on Kübelwagen chassis), and parts and materials were becoming scarce. That, along with fuel shortages, some were forced to convert their cars to run on propane or burn wood. On April 10, American troops marched into the KdF town of Fallersleben, where the factory had been heavily damaged after several Allied bombing raids had dumped thousands of pounds of high-explosive and incendiary bombs on and around the town the year before. However, one year later, most of the damage was still visible, as no appropriations had been taken to clean up the factory (after the war, a survey by the United States Strategic Bombing Survey team discovered that more than 38 percent of the factory's floor, or close to 2.8 million square feet, were rendered unusable). Of the 17,109 people living in Fallersleben at the time, more than 9000 were employed by Volkswagenwerk. Most were refugees fleeing from the eastern and western fronts of the war.

Soon after the American forces moved on, Britain occupied the plant and began using it as a vehicle repair depot. Under the control of Major Ivan Hirst, they soon permitted Germans to work in the factory again, and by May of 1945, they had produced two Volkswagen Beetles from various parts scattered around the wrecked factory buildings.

The 58 true Volkswagen Beetles produced in 1945 are not much different than their prewar counterparts. The all-steel bodies were from the same presses as the 1938 car except for the front inner stampings around the gas tank, the front axle and the louvers under the rear windows. It used the 1131cc, 25hp, horizontally opposed aircooled engine introduced in March 1943 for the Kübelwagen. It could be started from the inside using a key or from the outside with a hand crank.

Date	Chassis/Unit Numbers	Modification
May 16, 1945	052 016	**Body**: Chassis number inscribed (punched) by hand on the tunnel below rear seat.
1945	055 085	**Steering**: Gear box cover material changed from a light to a thicker metal.
1945	—/—	**Body:** Narrow bumpers and overriders were used. They were painted, not chrome.
1945	—/—	**Body:** Black Hella horn was mounted on a special bracket attached to the top of the driver's side bumper bracket
1945	—/—	**Interior:** Dropped plate with printed shift pattern on the center of the dash. Instead a VW emblem was part of the stamping.
1945	—/—	**Body:** Dropped the hubcaps in the early cars due to lack of materials.
1945	—/—	**Body:** Some early 1945–'45 models used several pieces of metal to form the various body panels.

1945

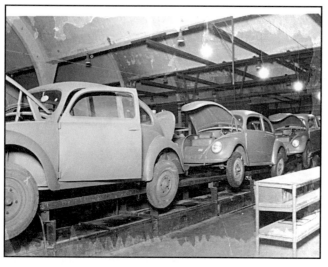

Production lines moved slowly soon after the war, as a short-age of material was a consistent problem for management.

Between the years 1945 and 1948, there are no physical changes to the bodywork, as Volkswagen was struggling to make cars with what materials they had. They weren't in the position to make unnecessary improvements.

Until 1951, the real axle employed single-action shock absorbers. Note the cutaway of the non-synchronized trans-mission.

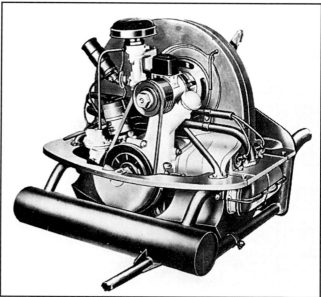

The famous 36hp engine in its stock, original form.

1946

Chassis Numbers: 053815 to 063796
Engine Numbers: 079093 to 090732
Produced between January 1, 1946 and December 31, 1946

Ivan Hirst's goal was to build 1000 Volkswagens a month in 1946, as most of these would go toward fulfilling the contract with the Allied forces. However, his goals were difficult to reach, as the simple act of feeding the workforce became a priority. In the harsh aftermath of war, the noontime lunch that Hirst provided was sometimes the only meal the workers got all day. At the end of the year, his goal was closely met. Of 10,020 Beetles produced that year, almost all of them were normal sedans. However, a few Kommandeurwagens had also been put together when the parts were available. There were little to no changes this year.

Date	Chassis/Unit Numbers	Modification
1946	054617	**Engine:** Corrugated tube ends fitted in cases instead of with springs.
1946	057390	**Chassis:** Fuel tank positioned higher on the chassis.
1946	057011	**Front:** Grease nipple moved to face left rear wheel.
1946	058568	**Front Axle:** reinforcing plates added to left and right side plates.
1946	054210	**Rear Axle:** The shaft spacer surface is now ground instead of turned.
1946	053107	**Brakes:** The cables are equipped with a grease nipple.
1946	059107	**Tires:** Increased tire size from 4.5 x 16 to 5.0 x 16.
1946	057893	**Engine:** Noise dampening cardboard added to engine compartment.

The interiors remained simple and practical, speedometer (and odometer) in the middle, flanked by a clock on the right and dual glove boxes on either side.

The post-war Beetle's engine had the coil mounted on the other side of the fan shroud.

1946

At the end of the war, to distance itself from the Nazi ties, the city of KdF-Wagen Stadt was renamed Wolfsburg, in honor of the castle nearby.

Volkswagens were used and abused by the occupying military personnel and sit here awaiting a rebuild (or to be used as a parts source).

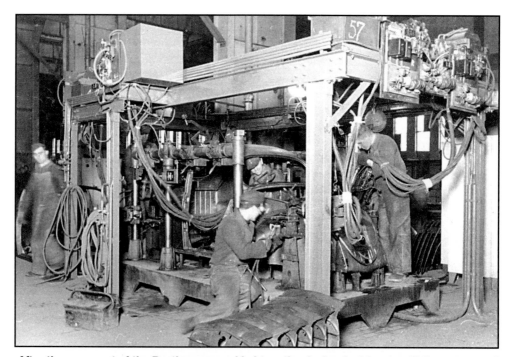

After the war, most of the Beetles were welded together by hand, at least until the automated welders could be reinstalled and/or repaired.

1947

Chassis Numbers: 063796 to 072743
Engine Numbers: 090732 to 0100788
Produced between January 1, 1947 and December 31, 1947

When the Beetle was displayed at the Hanover Fair in 1947, many people were excited to hear about when they could purchase one, as most all of the Beetles produced went to occupational forces and only a few actually ended up in the hands of private German citizens. Enter Ben Pon and his willingness to help in Volkswagen's infant export interests. He ordered six Beetles, and Volkswagen made sure that he included spare parts for a possible service support. All during this time, a percentage of the work force was still cleaning up the factory and repairing damage wrought on it during the war. Production of the Beetle actually fell during 1947, due to the lack of coal during the winter months, when production came to a halt for three months.

Date	Chassis/Unit Numbers	Modification
1947	071616/099610	**Engine**: The cooling air throttle ring changed to have a swing handle instead of a slide.
1947	064340/069102	**Front Axle**: The outside diameter for the ball bearing on the wheel hubs is increased from 52mm to 62mm.
1947	071478	**Front Axle**: The king pin bearing cap receives a modified bore.
1947	065866	**Rear Axle:** The bearing cover is secured by a hex head bolt and spring washer instead of hex socket screw.
1947	071595/079415	**Transmission**: The differential bearing seat is narrowed.
1947	071377	**Body**: Spare tire lock and chain are fixed on the body with an improved bracket.
October 13, 1947	072743	**Chassis**: The numbers are now punched in by stencil at the frame tunnel between shift lever and hand brake lever.

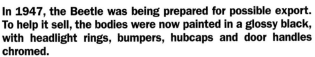

In 1947, the Beetle was being prepared for possible export. To help it sell, the bodies were now painted in a glossy black, with headlight rings, bumpers, hubcaps and door handles chromed.

Here Ben Pon (at left) and his staff pick up the first of five Beetles to be exported to Netherlands. Note there are six people in the photo, as he was supposed to pick up six, but one didn't pass inspection and was not permitted to leave the factory.

1948

Chassis Numbers: 072744 to 091921
Engine Numbers: 0100789 to 0122649
Produced between January 1, 1948 and December 31, 1948

Plans for a redesigned Beetle began in 1948, as Nordhoff took complete control of the factory and the Volkswagen's fate. A new form of currency was introduced in Germany this year, the Deutschmark replaced the Reichmark, and attempted to stimulate the economy. East and West Germany split up, and America helped West Germany through the Marshall Plan, pouring millions of dollars into the economy. Production of the Beetle more than doubled from the year before, rising to 19,244 units. Two coachbuilders came to the factory to help increase sales and interest in the little cars. Karmann factory began building convertibles and the Hebmüller factory started work on their famous cars. In the fall, owners of the Stamp Saver books together filed a class-action suit against Volkswagen in an attempt to obtain the VWs they were promised. It wasn't settled until 1961.

Date	Chassis/Unit Numbers	Modification
1948	073816	**Engine:** The choke control cable is no longer spring loaded.
April 1948	076722/105558	**Engine:** Flywheel centering lug and flywheel bore is changed to 48.5mm
1948	079503	**Front Axle:** A friction washer is added to the bearing cap.
1948	090690	**Steering:** A longitudinal groove is added on the steering column for steering lock.
1948	090784/100481	**Rear Axle:** The oil deflector and spacer are modified on the brake drum. The width of the spacer is increased from 12.9–13.1mm to 15.9–16.1mm.

The Beetles in 1948 were similar to previous years except for the large VW logo hubcaps.

Milestones, such as this photo celebrating the 100,000th engine being built, were being achieved rapidly as the popularity of the Beetle began to rise.

1948

A new engine being prepared for installation in a 1948 Beetle. Notice the handle on the fan shroud that can be turned either direction, one for summer driving (to allow more air across the heads) and one for winter driving (to restrict cooling air).

These Beetles are being gassed up outside the factory. They are headed for use with the German police department.

1949

Chassis Numbers: 091922 to 138554
Engine Numbers: 122650 to 169913
Produced between January 1, 1949 and December 31, 1949

In July of 1949, a new model was introduced that was designed for export: Export Model. Distinguished from the Standard model by its chrome-plated (and curved) bumpers, hub caps, headlamp rings and door handles. The interior differed slightly. Besides the two-spoke steering wheel, the dashboard came with a radio block-off plate so cutting the dashboard wasn't necessary if the owner (or dealer) wished to install a radio. The overall quality of material for the Export Model was better. The Beetle was offered with a high-gloss paint for the first time, and the front hood was released from the inside. The horn was relocated underneath the car's front fender instead of bolted to the front bumper bracket. This year, Karmann offered their four-seat Beetle Cabriolet, and the cost of the Export Model was 5450 DM.

Date	Chassis/Unit Numbers	Modification
January 5, 1949	091914	**Interior**: The heater was now controlled by two cables.
January 12, 1949	092498/123184	**Engine**: Oil pump cover is pressed from thicker sheet metal.
January 14, 1949	092918/123564	**Engine**: The pot shaped air cleaner gives way to a mushroom shaped air cleaner.
January 18, 1949	092879	**Fuel**: Tank tap formerly a cork seal now made of Thiokol.
January 18, 1949	93130/98705	**Chassis**: Floor plates are designed to allow a larger cavity underneath rear seat.
January 18, 1949	093270/124031	**Chassis**: The lower heater channel flap is now without a hinge.
January 25, 1949	093781	**Interior**: The front seat now has a straight backrest in place of an inclined design.
January 25, 1949	093834	**Fuel**: Instead of a circlip, the throttle control cable is fitted with an elbow at the front end.
January 28, 1949	093401/43150	**Chassis**: Fuel tank support lowered 4.5mm.
February 1, 1949	094554/125426	**Engine**: An intake manifold support is added.
February 9, 1949	094470/44221	**Interior**: When the backseat is down, two metal runners span the luggage compartment floor (lengthwise).
March 1949	—/—	**Steering**: Column tube now has a smaller inside diameter at the wheel.
March 7, 1949	096978/128051	**Engine**: The fan housing is now without throttle ring.
March 7, 1949	097121/107180	**Rear Axle**: The seal is now made of rubber and beveled 2.9–2.3mm.
March 15, 1949	097580/106047–107046	**Front Axle**: One torsion leaf was added on thebottom and removed from the top.
March 17, 1949	098400/108553	**Transmission**: Gearbox oil amount reduced from three liters to 2.5L.
March 28, 1949	099506	**Brakes**: Shoes are ground before assembly.
April 7, 1949	100615/131840	**Engine**: The V-belts get modified stickers and new markings.
April 8, 1949	100826/132017	**Fuel**: Fuel pump fitted with blue Solex membrane and four seals.
April 14, 1949	101322/110007	**Front Axle**: One torsion leaf was added on the bottom and removed from the top: now standard equipment.
April 26, 1949	102026/112521	**Transmission**: The case, formerly made of a magnesium-aluminum alloy is made of Elecktron.
April 28, 1949	101902/133131	**Exhaust**: Except for engines numbered 133634 through 133668, pressure plates are inserted in the exhaust valves.

1949

Date	Chassis/Unit Numbers	Modification
April 28, 1949	0102651	**Chassis**: The chassis number is now a seven-digit number.
May 1949	— /—	**Engine**: The V-Belts now have red markings for adjusting belt tension.
May 1, 1949	0102948/56912	**Interior**: Radio blank plate (Bakelite) is now made of plastic.
May 1, 1949	0102948/56912	**Body**: The front hood is equipped with a Bowden cable-type locking device (operated from inside the car) instead of a lockable handle.
May 1, 1949	0102948/56912	**Body**: The deck lid is no longer lockable.
May 6, 1949	10105848/56612	**Electrical**: The fuse box is moved from underneath the instrument panel to the left of the instrument panel.
May 6, 1949	10406483/56078	**Electrical**: The stop light bulb is now six-volts and 15 watts.
May 6, 1949	0102383/52070	**Interior**: For the Export Model, the dashboard is completely reworked, including a clock and the two-spoke (batwing) steering wheel.
May 6, 1949	103039/109131	**Heating**: The control cable guide tube now has a rubber plug.
May 6, 1949	103610/114140	**Transmission**: The mounting bracket now has a center marking.
May 9, 1949	103188	**Fuel**: Tank strainer is fitted with triple wire netting.
May 9, 1949	103610/114140	**Transmission**: Instead of a center marking, the mounting bracket now has a 3mm indentation.
May 9, 1949	0103800/53453	**Interior**: The glove compartment, previously made of molded sheet metal, is now plastic and is secured with a strap.
May 9, 1949	0103889/53517	**Interior**: The rear seat back stops have been relocated 30mm to the rear (results in more inclined position).
May 23, 1949	0105290	**Chassis**: The grease nipples are no longer marked red.
June 1949	— /—	**Interior**: The rearview mirror is made of plate glass instead of sheet glass and has a vibration-free mounting.
June 6, 1949	0099906	**General**: Production begins on the VW Beetle Convertible.
June 1949	106637/137701	**Engine**: The vent pipe is extended
June 2, 1949	0106636	**Body**: The nitro (cellulose)-based paint is dropped in favor of a synthetic resin-based paint.
June 2, 1949	0106636	**General**: The Export Sedan model production begins.
June 22, 1949	107101/115523	**Chassis**: The frame number is now punched in with stencil in longitudinal direction into the flat surface of the frame tunnel.
June 1949	0108091/139293	**Engine**: Cylinder ventilation holes now have caps.
June 1949	0108344/177059	**Front Axle**: Bearing caps are now without top cover plate, and the link pin bushing's outer grease groove is no longer provided. Grease nipple is relocated.
June 1949	0108745/119201	**Rear Axle**: The oil seal is now made of Perbunan and is blue.
July 1949	0111054/60759	**Body**: The pressed-in recess for the license plate on the deck lid is no longer provided.
July 1949	0111255/60869	**Interior**: The support strap for the glove compartment is deleted.
July 1949	0114186	**Engine**: Felt cone filter added.
August 1949	115763/126067	**Brakes**: The backing plate now has four long holes.
August 1949	116920/127189	**Rear Axle**: The bearing flange is now secured with a splined dowel pin, where a hex bolt and nut had been used.

1949

Date	Chassis/Unit Numbers	Modification
August 1949	116375/116021	**Fuel**: The shape of the tank is modified, the tap is located in the center and the filter is discontinued.
August 1949	0116616	**Body**: The windshield transfer picture with running-in instructions is no dropped.
August 1949	116811/147950	**Engine**: The connecting rod bushings are widened.
August 1949	117053	**Suspension**: Lever-type shock absorber is changed from single action to double action on some models.
August 1949	117053/125338	**Suspension**: The axle tubes and torsion bars are shortened.
August 1949	117389/148542	**Fuel**: Solex fuel pump now standard.
August 1949	117469	**Brakes**: The brakes now have stronger down gearing.
August 1949	0117700/67337	**Interior**: The left door arm rest is no longer provided.
September 1949	119364/150486	**Fuel**: Solex carburetor now standard.
September 1949	119588/150702	**Engine**: Piston clearance 0.05mm larger for third piston.
September 1949	120959/152050	**Transmission**: Radially ribbed clutch disc with double thrust springs are now used.
September 1949	123476/131907	**Front Axle**: Left-hand and right-hand threads on the tie rods now standard equipment.
September 30, 1949	142902	**Engine**: Cylinders are made with a higher phosphorus content.
October 1949	— /—	**Tools**: Starting handle discontinued.
October 1949	0124032/73554	**Interior**: The front rubber mats are now in a brown/beige color while the rear mats are no longer provided.
October 1949	0124250/73837	**Body**: The front hood lock is now equipped with a cover plate.
October 1949	125054	**Chassis**: Anti-vibration agent is sprayed on.
October 1949	0125707/74755	**Interior**: The coat hook is now part of a threaded plate welded into the inner side panel.
October 1949	126157	**Brakes**: The cables are now coated with a Mipolam sheathing.
October 1949	127560/137582	**Transmission**: Clutch lever is reinforced.
October 1949	128058	**Interior**: The accelerator pedal's roller is now larger.
October 1949	128116	**Interior**: The seat runner on the driver's side is raised 15mm.
November 1949	127600	**Suspension**: Lever-type shock absorber is alternatively Boge or Hemscheidt, where Hemscheidt had been used exclusively.
November 1949	129619/136360	**Chassis**: Anti-vibration agent discontinued.
November 1949	131890/140456	**Suspension**: Front shock absorbers are now marked blue (high pressure) and yellow (low pressure).
November 1949	0133399	**Interior**: The door lock is operated by a pull rod with an elongated covering.
December 1949	133888/143905	**Transmission**: The case has a wide differential ball bearing seat on right and left side, whereas before there was only a narrow seat on the right-hand side.
December 1949	137970	**Suspension**: The lever-type shock absorber links are now twisted bands instead of a straight band.

1949

The 1949 Beetle, the first year of significant change.

The first Karmann-prepared four-seat convertibles were being produced. They used the 1948 large-VW-logo hubcaps for the first few months of production.

The Export Model dashboard was equipped with a glove box and instrument panels ringed in chrome. The two-spoke steering wheel (batwing) and control knobs were ivory in color.

By comparison, here is the Standard Model dashboard. Note the lack of chrome attributes. Instead of cutting the dash if a radio is to be installed, a block-off plate is attached.

The rear deck lid no longer has a separate pressing for the license plate. As well, the lid can no longer be locked.

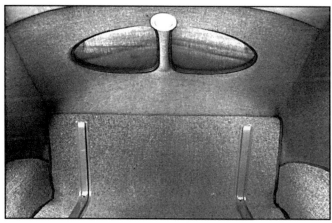

The luggage compartment of a 1949 Beetle with the addition of two longitudinal metal rails.

1949

On top of the 1100cc engine is the new "mushroom"-shape air filter of 1949.

With the body removed, it is easy to see the front beam, the steering box and the smaller roller ball throttle pedal, used until October 1949.

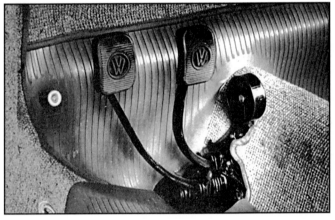

In contrast, the large roller ball throttle pedal from October 1949.

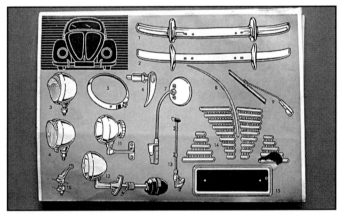

Dress up items were available to new VW owners as displayed in this parts brochure.

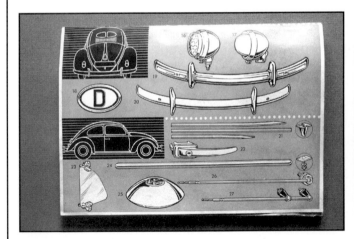

Fog lights, new chrome trim and antennas made each car look separate from the rest.

Early accessories were available either from the factory or from the dealer. Items such as cleaning brushes, mirrors, tool kits and bud vases could be purchased.

1950

Chassis Numbers: 138555 to 220133
Engine Numbers: 169914 to 265999
Produced between January 1, 1950 and December 31, 1950

This is the first year the "folding" sunroof is offered, so named by VW specialist Arthur Westrup in his 1950 book *Drive Better with the Volkswagen*. The cost for the folding sunroof was an additional 250 DM. As well, notched door window glass was added to help in cabin ventilation. Hydraulic brakes were added to the Export Model.

In the Volkswagen factory, 342 Beetles are produced daily, and in March, the 13,505 workers celebrated the production of the 100,000th Beetle. Volkswagens accounted for 41.5 percent of all cars registered in Germany in 1950, and Volkswagen employees enjoy the above-average pay scale, with an hourly wage of 1.50 DM, versus the national average of 1.24 DM. In addition, Volkswagen begins production of its second line of cars, the Transporter, with full-scale production beginning March 8, 1950.

Date	Chassis/Unit Numbers	Modification
January 1950	1-0138646/169969	**Engine**: The oil filler and breather assembly is now fitted with a gasket.
January 1950	1-0140537/89656	**Electrical**: The control lights for the instrument panel are redesigned.
January 1950	1-0142069/152405	**Transmission**: Now used Hypoid oil.
January 4, 1950	1-0139264/147790	**Front Axle**: The Pitman arm is now fitted with a shorter-thread hex bolt.
January 1950	1-0138765/17086	**Engine**: The oil can now be completely drained thanks to a passage through the timing gear chamber. Oil quantity: 2.5L. The fourth main bearing bore now has a groove, and an oil deflector is no longer needed.
January 1950	1-0140130/89257	**Body**: The hood locking button is enlarged.
January 1950	1-0140243	**Engine**: There is now a gasket between the cylinder and the cylinder head.
January 17, 1950	1-0141601/173030	**Engine**: The dipstick is treated with a phosphoric acid and blackened.
January 16, 1950	1-0141236	**Engine**: The exhaust pipe flanges are now surface ground.
January 21, 1950	1-0142442/173950	**Engine**: The welded seam on the induction tube between the intake manifold and the preheating pipe is extended 10mm on both sides.
January 26, 1950	1-0143276/92290	**Body**: The fenders are equipped with a ring seal between the headlight and fender.
January 27, 1950	1-0143592/153800	**Transmission**: The case now has 0.10–0.18mm contact stress between ball bearings and differential housing.
February 1950	—/—	**Transmission**: The oil drain plug is decreased from 22mm to 19mm.
February 7, 1950	1-0145428/94350	**Fuel**: The tank filler cap is now fitted with a strainer in 16,000 cars.
February 10, 1950	1-0146222	**Fuel**: The throttle control cable is switched from an elbow to a pin and loop at the front end.
February 12, 1950	1-0149061	**Engine**: The oil drain plug is now a 19mm hex head on all models.
February 13, 1950	1-0146657/95531	**Interior**: A brown/beige-colored rubber mat is added to the rear hair cord carpet set.
March 1950	—/—	**Tools**: The spark plug wrench is now a "Special Hazet 500."

1950

Date	Chassis/Unit Numbers	Modification
March 1950	—/—	**Fuel**: The fuel pump is now fitted with a black flexible diaphragm.
March 14, 1950	1-0152827/101560	**Interior**: The rear side paneling is now made of water-resistant oil paper.
March 14, 1950	1-0152857/185196	**Engine**: "KS" pistons, with a 0.035 to 0.055mm clearance, are used exclusively from now on.
March 24, 1950	1-0155020/103707	**Electrical**: Volkswagen begins using Bosch headlamps instead of their own brand.
March 30, 1950	1-0156129/188974	**Exhaust**: The exhaust pipe diameter is increased by one millimeter to 32mm.
April 3, 1950	1-0145970/189691	**Engine**: The intake manifold and preheating pipe receive a light metal jacket to increase preheating of fuel/air mixture.
April 1950	1-0158253	**Brakes**: Hydraulic brakes now standard.
April 18, 1950	1-0159782/108281	**Interior**: The pin in the left door latch mechanism no longer provided while the right side has a lockable handle.
April 21, 1950	1-0160382/172207	**Transmission**: The case seal is increased in thickness from 0.10mm to 0.25–0.30mm.
April 25, 1950	1-0161234/194696	**Fuel**: The Solex carburetor's float is now hinged and weighs 12.5 g. The pilot jet is 1mm in diameter.
April 29, 1950	1-0162444	**Heating**: The control knob is rotary.
May 1950	—/—	**Transmission**: Now only Gleason or Klingelnberg gear wheels are used.
May 4, 1950	1-0161311/109663	**Exhaust**: Noise muffler is now standard.
May 9, 1950	1-0164280	**Brakes**: Hand brake now has a beam-shaped support head.
May 13, 1950	—/199321	**Engine**: Mahle Autothermik pistons are now used in a number of engine cases.
May 13, 1950	1-0164460	**Brakes**: Fluid reservoir now has a float instead of a filter/strainer.
May 16, 1950	1-0166185/174820	**Steering**: The thrust spring force is reduced by approximately one-third.
May 20, 1950	1-0167890	**Brakes**: Master cylinder diameter reduces from 22.2mm to 19.5mm, while the rear brake cylinder is increased from 15.9mm to 19.05mm.
June 1950	1-0169704/204025	**Engine**: The valve seat ring is made of V2A steel.
June 3, 1950	1-0169714/114146	**Interior**: Ashtrays are added on the instrument panel and right rear quarter panel.
June 6, 1950	1-0167213	**Exhaust**: An Eberspacker make muffler is used on the convertible only.
June 1950	1-0172368	**Engine**: The inner half of the pulley now has a spot-welded spacer.
June 1950	1-0173719/108481	**Transmission**: The clutch now only uses one spring.
June 27, 1950	1-0175999	**Front Axle**: The ball diameter is increased by 2mm.
July 1950	1-0177736	**Fuel**: The carburetor is without a hinged float on 154 cases (213301–213455).

1950

Date	Chassis/Unit Numbers	Modification
August 2, 1950	1-0181877	**Interior**: The glove box is sprayed with a wool and silk dust mixture instead of a cloth lining.
August 1950	1-183052/125336	**Suspension**: The front shock absorbers (Hemscheidt) are equipped with a fluid reservoir.
August 10, 1950	1-0183539/220317	**Exhaust**: The valve metal is hardened.
August 11, 1950	—/—	**Interior**: The accelerator pedal is attached using a pin instead of a screw.
August 28, 1950	1-0188291	**Engine**: Nural pistons (75mm) are used on engine cases 225484–226410.
September 30, 1950	1-0194649/216225	**Transmission**: The engaging notches for the shift rod for third and fourth gears now has a shallow seat.
October 1950	—/—	**Engine**: The oil filter is now a mechanic part.
October 1950	1-0195789/285789	**Engine**: The V-belt is now an 875 cable-corded belt.
October 17, 1950	1-0202071	**Brakes**: The hand brake lever is shorter.
November 16, 1950	1-0210371	**Exhaust**: The valves have welded tips on engine cases 252725–253775.

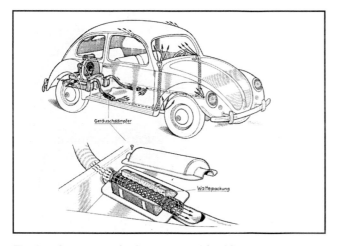

The heating system is demonstrated in this sales literature drawing, and a detailed cutaway of the rear passenger floor heating vent noise mufflers is included.

This woman shows off her new Beetle for the camera. This is clearly a European model because of the lack of overriders on the front bumper.

1951

Chassis Numbers: 220134 to 313829
Engine Numbers: 266000 to 379470
Produced between January 1, 1951 and December 31, 1951

In 1951, the cheapest Volkswagen Beetle was 4600 DM. There were 93,709 of them made, and of those 35,742 were exported to 29 different countries. The largest number of buyers were in Belgium, Sweden, Switzerland, Holland, Finland and Brazil. In Germany, there were now 729 Volkswagen service stations, employing 11,121 mechanics. The Standard Model came only in Mid-Blue and Pearl Grey; seventy-five percent of all new buyers chose Grey. The Export Model was distinguished by the side ventilation flaps in the front quarter panels as well as the decorative chrome around the front windshield and Wolfsburg crest on the front hood trim. In the rear seats, the cushions were removed after Volkswagen officials commented that, "they gave the passengers the feeling of being in a boudoir."

Date	Chassis/Unit Numbers	Modification
January 4, 1951	1-0221051/266644	**Engine**: The belt pulley has a modified shim with an outer diameter of 4mm and an inner of 3mm (decreasing both by one mm).
January 6, 1951	1-0221638/168482	**Body**: Ventilation flaps are fitted on the front side panels.
January 18, 1951	1-0224171/270484	**Engine**: The crank case is made of Elektron instead of a magnesium-aluminum alloy.
January 22, 1951	1-0225511	**Fuel**: The pin for the throttle control cable increases in diameter from 2.1mm to 2.2mm.
February 5, 1951	1-0229182	**General**: The VW Standard Beetle is "run in" tested on a test bench rather than on the road.
February 13, 1951	1-0231453/259012	**Transmission**: The reverse pin is a C-washer and pin with an angular groove instead of a stop.
February 15, 1951	—/—	**Heating**: An additional notch for an intermediate stage has been added to the control cable.
March 19, 1951	1-0240961/250713	**Front Axle**: The king pins are equipped with outer lubrication grooves.
March 21, 1951	1-0241734/287661	**Engine**: The camshaft gear is made of "Resitax" plastic on the Export models.
March 27, 1951	1-0242600/293200	**Exhaust**: The muffler pipe is modified.
April 1, 1951	1-0243731	**Body**: The front hood on the Export model now sports the Wolfsburg crest.
April 1, 1951	1-0243731	**Body**: The rear quarter panels have higher supports, giving greater tire clearance.
April 6, 1951	1-0244003/274520	**Suspension**: The lever shock absorber gives way to a telescopic shock absorber (for Export and Cabrio models only).
April 6, 1951	1-0244003/274520	**Brakes**: The rear wheel back plates are interchangeable, while cables for the hand brake are no longer used.
April 12, 1951	1-0244668	**Body**: The windshield now has chrome trim. Ventilation flaps are fitting on the front left and right side panels. A Bowden cable is used to release the trunk as opposed to a latch. The glove box is now lockable on the convertible model.

1951

Date	Chassis/Unit Numbers	Modification
April 13, 1951	1-0241638	**Interior**: Door panels come with one side pocket on the convertible model.
April 18, 1951	1-0246090/297815	**Engine**: The generator is upgraded from AL 15 to RED 130/6-2600 AL16.
April 1951	—/—	**Steering**: A reinforced spring is added to the damper.
April 1951	—/296606	**Engine**: Openings are provided in both sides of the crank case halves for lubrication.
May 25, 1951	1-0253756	**Electrical**: The starter wire is lengthened by 100mm, and is extended downward from the side of the battery cover instead of straight back toward the rear.
May 25, 1951	1-0253756	**Transmission**: The clutch cable is arranged to travel straight through the cross members instead of at an arc.
July 10, 1951	1-0266453/301644	**Transmission**: The differential side and bevel gears use Klingelberg or Gleason teeth. The bevel gear teeth reduce in number from 13 to 11, while the side gear teeth reduce from 20 to 17 in number.
July 31, 1951	1-0272406	**Brakes**: The hand brake lever is covered by a rubber sleeve at frame tunnel.
August 1, 1951	1-0272706/330345	**Engine**: The oil breather is equipped with a filler cap and clamp spring.
August 6, 1951	1-0274656	**Brakes**: The rubber sleeve at frame tunnel for the hand brake lever is no longer provided.
August 14, 1951	1-0276126/276126	**Interior**: The ventilation shutters now have a wire screen and an operating lever.
August 21, 1951	1-0278121/336759	**Engine**: The cylinder head cover plate is made of one piece.
September 19, 1951	1-0286202/230356	**Body:** The running board trim is now attached by clips instead of screws.
September 24, 1951	1-0287416	**Tools**: The wheel bolts are no longer included in the tool kit.
October 25, 1951	1-0296592/302965	**Body**: The jack mounting points are reinforced.
November 6, 1951	1-0299992/312446	**Front Axle:** The tie rods now have angular grease nipples instead of straight ones.
November 19, 1951	1-0303920/316455	**Steering**: The thread pitch for the gear case is lowered.
November 20, 1951	1-0304210	**Interior**: The rear seat arm rest cushions no longer provided.
November 26, 1951	1-0305813/369483	**Exhaust**: The exhaust valve seat ring is now made of V2A steel.
November 28, 1951	1-0306724/348990	**Rear Axle**: The pinion nut tightening instructions are now first tighten with 15mkg of torque, loosen, then tighten with 5mkg.
December 1, 1951	10308653	**Electrical**: The wattage of the instrument panel light is increased from 0.6 to 1.2 watts.
December 5, 1951	1-0308242	**Rear Axle**: The pinion assembly and cylinder roller bearings are now dipped in 90-degree Celsius oil before assembling.
December 10, 1951	1-0309480	**Steering**: The dimensions of the gear case decreased from 37/35mm to 32/30mm to prevent loss of oil.

1951

Date	Chassis/Unit Numbers	Modification
December 10, 1951	1-0309833	Engine: The throttle hole diameter (through butterfly) on the Solex carburetor (26 VFIS) is now 1.4–1.5mm.
December 17, 1951	1-0311923/376900	Fuel: The throttle ring is now spot welded instead of screwed.

The 1951 Beetle had front quarter panel vents for great cooling ability during hot summer months.

The symmetrical layout of the dashboard permitted the factory to install the steering wheel on either side, depending on the requirements of the country it was destined for.

Only on the Export Model and the Convertible have the single-action shock absorbers been replaced with double-action, telescopic shocks.

Under the rear seat, the batteries are secured via two springs which clip onto hooks on the lid. Before, this was a source of fire, as the cover was merely made of cardboard and was subjected to the acids of the battery.

1952

Chassis Numbers: 1-0313830 to 1-0428156
Engine Numbers: 379471 to 519136
Produced between January 1, 1952 and December 31, 1952

Most noteworthy of cars made in 1952 were the addition of the vent wing windows in the front doors. This allowed for an adjustable increase in airflow. The bumpers had two impact-resistant overriders, and the horn grills were now round and painted to match the rest of the car (on the Standard Model). The Export Model was outfitted with much more chrome/aluminum trim on the doors, side panels, side and rear windows and horn grills. The deck lid handle was redesigned, and the dashboard was transformed, so that there was a glove box and the starter button and turn signal switch were located on the left of the steering wheel (and the choke was on the right). The interior light was moved from the rear (between the split windows) to the B-pillar above the door. The Export Model had a black horn button with a gold Wolfsburg crest, and the lights and wipers were activated by pull switches. For better preheating of the air/fuel mixture, an exhaust heater tube contacted the inlet manifold. On the Export Model, second, third and fourth gears are synchromeshed, and the ride was improved by a new six-leaf torsion bar system in the front.

Of all the Beetles made in 1952, 41.4 percent were exported, and toward the end of the year, the daily production numbers increased to 734. Contrary to the previous year, the most expensive Beetle was 4600 DM.

Date	Chassis/Unit Numbers	Modification
January 15, 1952	1-0317628/323737	**Steering**: The steering wheel nut is made of bronze and the play is changed to 0.1-0.2mm.
January 21, 1952	1-0320804	**Engine**: The thermostat now has a simplified holder.
January 21, 1952	1-0320804	**Engine**: A felt ring seal is added to the gland nut to prevent loss of grease.
January 22, 1952	1-0316900	**Brakes**: The hand brake lever now has a covering at the frame tunnel (For Export Models only).
January 26, 1952	1-0318328	**Brakes**: Instead of two returns springs, the front and rear brakes use only one spring, and the angle brackets are no longer provided.
January 31, 1952	1-0322465	**Steering**: The lockable steering column is no longer standard equipment.
February 4, 1952	1-0323508	**Body**: The engine seal guide is recessed for easier engine removal.
February 7, 1952	1-0324532/392231	**Engine**: The upper air duct lateral support is no longer fitted.
February 15, 1952	1-0325623/338524	**Suspension**: The torsion arms and bushings play was increased from 0.10–0.17mm to 0.15–0.22mm.
February 15, 1952	1-0326816/372084	**Transmission**: The reverse sliding gear is beveled from 29.1/28.9mm to 27.5/27.3mm.
February 21, 1952	1-0328831/397264	**Engine**: The intake and exhaust valve cams are modified to reduce noise.
February 20, 1952	1-0322639	**Electrical**: The parking light within the headlight changes terminals, from 58 to 57.
March 3, 1952	1-0331416	**Body**: The sliding sunroof transition is modified at the guide bow ends.
March 4, 1952	1-0331701/400705	**Engine**: The cover plates between the lower heater channels are no longer fitted.
March 19, 1952	1-0336561	**Tools**: The jack is now a Klettermaxe type.
March 21, 1952	1-0336403/349482	**Steering**: Before they were welded together, but now the shaft and steering column are made of one piece.
March 25, 1952	1-0338059/408661	**Exhaust**: The connecting pipe between the exhaust pipe and

1952

Date	Chassis/Unit Numbers	Modification
		muffler is no longer fitted.
April 22, 1952	1-0345950/358997	**Front Axle**: The pitman arm is now reinforced on all left-hand-drive cars.
May 14, 1952	1-0353634	**Interior**: The glove compartment is now lined with gray and beige velvet instead of sprayed wool dust.
May 29, 1952	1-0357667/433003	**Engine**: There are now two valve springs instead of one.
June 7, 1952	1-0360478/436414	**Engine**: The dipstick tube is relocated to a higher position.
June 9, 1952	1-0360851/436869	**Engine:** The fan wheel balance center is relocated.
June 23, 1952	1-0365716	**Body**: The cover and opening in luggage compartment floor (for access to the transmission) no longer offered.
June 30, 1952	1-0368508	**Engine**: The V-belt is made from "Optiflex" material.
July 29, 1952	1-0374199/414689	**Fuel**: The filler neck diameter is reduced from 100mm to 60mm.
August 20, 1952	1-0382029/462001	**Engine**: An oil bath cleaner is fitted on some models.
September 18, 1952	1-0391619/473814	**Transmission:** The clutch plate (now 1.2mm) features a "Textar" lining only.
September 26, 1952	1-0395819	**Engine**: The flywheel's radial run-out is limited to 0.2mm.
September 30, 1950	1-0396588/456170	**Transmission**: The gear shift housing is supported by two reinforcing ribs on the bottom instead of one on the top.
October 1, 1952	—/—	**Rear Axle**: The unit number (now starting with A-00001) is now located on the right half of the gear shift housing in front of the contact plate.
October 1, 1952	—/—	**Rear Axle**: The diameter of torsions bars is decreased from 25mm to 24mm.
October 1, 1952	1-0397023/481713	**Tools**: The extra V-belt is no longer available in the tool kit.
October 1, 1952	1-0397023	**Transmission**: Fitted to the Export Sedan is a synchronized transmission (2nd, 3rd and 4th) instead of a standard transmission. Mounting points are a softer three-point rubber suspension.
October 1, 1952	1-0397023/481713	**Heating**: The heater can now be fine adjusted by a rotary knob and spindle.
October 1, 1952	1-0397023/481713	**Fuel**: The 26 VPIS carburetor is upgraded by the use of a 28 PCI model.
October 1, 1952	1-0397023/481713	**Front Axle**: The torsion bars now use six springs.
October 1, 1952	1-0397023/481713	**Suspension:** The shock absorber travel is decreased from 130mm to 90mm.
October 1, 1952	1-0397023/481713	**Fuel**: The fuel pipe cross section is decreased from 32mm to 17mm.
October 1, 1952	1-0397023	**Tires/Rims**: The tire size is changed from 5.00 x 16 to 5.60 x 15 and the rims are 4.5 x 15. Tire pressure is now 1.1kg/sq.cm. in front and 1.4-1.6kg/sq.cm.in rear.
October 1, 1952	1-0397023	**Interior**: The mirror becomes more rounded. The seats get reinforced

1952

Date	Chassis/Unit Numbers	Modification
		springs and improved backrest shape. Vent wings are added to both doors. The defroster nozzles for the windshield are wider. The number of turns to roll down the windows is decreased from 10.5 to 3.25 revolutions. The glovebox receives a cover and push button. Instrument panel is redesigned, including an ashtray for front seat passenger. The floor mats are now slip-proof by being secured with press buttons.
October 1, 1952	1-0397023	**Engine**: Cardboard noise dampening material is added to the engine compartment.
October 1, 1952	1-0397023	**Electrical**: There are now two lateral lamps combined with the taillight and reflectors. The fuse box for stop and taillights is now underneath the instrument panel instead of in the engine compartment. The windshield wipers are now fitted with an electronic return (on Export Model). The starter button is on the left of the steering column instead of on the right. Five kilograms of pressure is required to activate the dimmer switch instead of eight kilograms of pressure. A lever on the left-hand side of the steering column is now used to activate the turn signals instead of a switch on the dashboard. The rotary switches for the headlights and windshield wipers are replaced by pull switches. The dome light between the split windows is replaced by a light above the driver's door. Formerly mounted on top of the bumper bracket, the horn is now concealed beneath a ornamental grill. The horn button now has a coat of arms printed on it.
October 1, 1952	1-0397023	**Body**: The bumpers have a wider profile and stronger overriders, and the moldings are now anodized polished metal.
October 15, 1952	1-0402005	**Rear Axle:** The shock absorber uses a longer hex bolt, 22mm long.
October 15, 1952	1-0402111	**Tools:** The extra V-belt is again available in the tool kit.
October 16, 1952	1-0402727	**Transmission:** The shift sleeve for 3rd and 4th gears are 0.6mm wider.
November 1952	—/—	**Engine:** The felt cone air cleaner is now equipped with a flame guard screen.
November 1, 1952	1-0397023	**Transmission:** Second, third and fourth gears are synchromeshed on all export models.
November 13, 1952	—/—	**Trunk:** A noise dampening felt mat is available in the convertible's luggage compartment.
November 14, 1952	—/—	**Body:** Side moldings are attached by modified clamps and holes.
November 24, 1952	1-0416104	**Rear Axle:** The hand brake cable receives a rubber tube to prevent rattling on the Export models.
November 26, 1952	1-0423415/513320	**Engine:** The diameter of the intake valve decreases from 5.075 to 4.9.
December 3, 1952	1-0419133/508079	**Engine:** The diameter of the right heater channel linkage is modified from 207.5mm to 203.5mm, and the right side changed from 221.5mm to 217.5mm.
December 12, 1952	1-0423119	**Fuel:** The choke control cable is protected by a Mipolam hose between frame and engine (670mm long).
December 14, 1952	—/—	**Chassis:** The frame numbers now start with KD instead of KT.

1952

Date	Chassis/Unit Numbers	Modification
December 16, 1952	1-0424308	**Interior**: The backs of the front seats receive cardboard protection.
December 30, 1952	1-0427392	**Body**: The tires have improved clearance because of a 5mm shorter support at the body (for snow chains).

The twin rear windows would only remain until March of the following year, and the redesigned Beetle now features vent windows, oval horn grills and 15-inch wheels.

The completely new dashboard for the 1952 year, with the glove box located on the far right and the left-hand box removed altogether.

1952

The starter button and turn signal switch were moved to the left-hand side. The turn signal switch is relocated to the steering column. The new speedometers had a 110mm diameter and warning lights are built in.

The horn button of the Export Model is black with a gold Wolfsburg crest, offset by a chrome-plated ring.

The heart-shaped taillights for braking was just one of a few added safety features on the 1952 Beetle. The backup lights were not standard for this year.

The engine comes equipped with a 28PCI carburetor and a choke for the first time.

1953

Chassis Numbers: 1-0428157 to 1-0579682
Engine Numbers: 519137 to 700697
Produced between January 1, 1953 and December 31, 1953

Through the course of the history of the Beetle, there are a few significant dates to highlight. One of them in particular is March 10, 1953. This day, the last Split Window Volkswagen (1-0454950) and the first Oval Window Volkswagen (1-0454951) were made side-by-side. The new window was 23 percent larger. An interesting side-note is the reason for the Split Window in the first place. Some have suggested that the Split Window and the center rib that splits the two windows were designed for strength and durability, while the real reason was that it was simply cheaper to make two smaller windows than one larger one. It was also in response to complaints from owners about a lack of visibility.

When the 500,000th Volkswagen rolled off the production line on July 3, 1953, the employees were given a 2.5 million marks bonus to split. 68,754 Beetles are exported, and Volkswagen had 42.5 percent of the domestic German market. The average daily production, including Transporters, was 673 vehicles.

Volkswagen de Brasil SA is formed in Sao Paulo, and on December 8, the 250,000th visitor (since the end of the war) comes to tour the Wolfsburg factory and its 20,569 employees.

Date	Chassis/Unit Numbers	Modification
January 1, 1953	1-0440292	**Suspension**: The front shock absorber (Boge model) now has a groove-type oil passage at piston.
January 6, 1953	1-0428157	**Body**: The rear bumper brackets are modified.
January 7, 1953	1-0430467	**Interior**: The floor carpet is attached with press buttons and is flatter.
January 15, 1953	1-0433397	**Fuel**: The carburetor's air correction jet is now 200 instead of 190.
January 20, 1953	1-0435509	**Engine**: The valve clearance is changed from 0.15mm to 0.10mm.
January 21, 1953	1-0435491	**Engine**: The oil cooler dampening plate offset is changed for noise reduction.
February 1953	—/—	**Suspension**: The front torsion arm diameter is reduced by 0.5mm.
February 2, 1953	1-0440717	**Body**: The sliding sunroof has chrome-plated guides, dampening pads and guide bars with plastic fillers.
February 13, 1953	1-0444803	**Engine**: The carburetor and fuel pump nipple angle is changed from 60 degrees to 45 degrees.
February 17, 1953	1-0446526	**Transmission**: The clutch lobes are increased from three to nine to improve centering.
February 27, 1953	1-0450810	**Transmission**: Oil capacity increased from 2.5L to 3.0L.
March 7, 1953	1-0454951	**Fuel**: The filler neck diameter increases from 40mm to 80mm.
March 10, 1953	1-0545951	**Body**: The moldings are now made of Reflectal. The rearview window is increased by 23 percent and is oval.The familiar "Split Window" design gives way to the "Oval Window" with a 23 percent increase in glass, and safety glass is now used.
March 10, 1953	1-0545951	**Interior**: The ashtrays now have handles and are located on the instrument panel.
March 20, 1953	1-0459217	**Fuel**: The choke control cable receives a Mipolam sheathing for the entire length and the guide tube increases from 8 x 1mm to 10 x 1mm.
April 11, 1953	1-0468206	**Steering**: The steering wheel's bushings are cast-in steel instead of pressed-on steel.

1953

Date	Chassis/Unit Numbers	Modification
May 1, 1953	—/—	**Engine**: The fuel pump flange's inside fins are reinforced to 2.5mm and the pressing temperature is increased to 170 degrees Celsius.
May 26, 1953	1-0485001	**Engine**: The thickness of the throttle control cable collar decreases from 3.0mm to 2.0mm.
May 28, 1953	1-0487128	**Engine**: The gland nut bushing is now made of brass instead of iron.
June 2, 1953	1-0448171	**Rear Axle**: The outside diameter of the rear wheel bearing spacer increased from 44.0/43.9mm to 44.5/44.4mm.
June 15, 1953	1-0494340	**Engine**: The ball valves on the Solex 28 PCI carburetor are now made of bronze instead of steel, and the pump channel is accessible through a screw plug instead of a steel pin tap.
June 18, 1953	1-0495968	**Electrics**: The windshield wiper shaft is lowered by 8mm, and the rubber seal for the wiper shafts is installed with sealing compound.
June 18, 1953	1-0495968	**Body**: The front hood hinge angle is reduced, and the lid bracket is shorter.
July 6, 1953	1-0503371	**Body**: The vent windows now have locks on the Export Model (from 1-0503276 for the Standard Model).
July 1953	1-0509668	**Interior**: The rearview mirror is now mounted with two rivets.
August 20, 1953	1-0517200	**Interior**: The knob for the heat control cable now has a flattened bottom.
August 20, 1953	1-0517304	**Front Axle**: The torsion bars now have eight leaves instead of six.
August 21, 1953	1-0517880	**Front Axle**: The front wheel bearing caps are no longer filled with grease.
August 31, 1953	1-0522314	**Engine**: The spark plug torque is increased from 4–5mkg to 7–7.5mkg.
September 29, 1953	1-0536041	**Brakes**: The front brakes cotter pin hole diameter decreases from 5.4/4.5mm to 5.0/4.5mm.
September 30, 1953	1-0536445	**Front Axle**: The front beam now has sheet metal below the frame end plate, and spot welding is replaced by projection welding.
October 14, 1953	1-0537356	**Engine**: The fan now has 1.5mm-thick blades instead of 1.25mm.
October 31, 1953	1-0552150	**Engine**: The surface to mark engine numbers is raised 2mm.
November 2, 1953	1-551808	**Wheels**: The metal thickness of the wheel plates is increased from 2.75mm to 3.0mm.
November 3, 1953	1-0552991	**Interior**: The heating control knob is now without lettering on the Standard model.
November 17, 1953	1-0559131	**Interior**: The heating control knob is now without lettering on the Export model.
November 21, 1953	1-0562054	**Steering**: The steering wheel now has two spokes pointed upward so as not to block the speedometer.
November 26, 1953	1-0564030	**Steering**: The maximum play is reduced to 3mm.
December 1, 1953	—/—	**Fuel**: The fuel cap spring tension is reduced to make it easier to open and close tank.

1953

Date	Chassis/Unit Numbers	Modification
December 21, 1953	1-0575415	**Engine:** The introduction of the 30hp 1192cc engine replaces the 35hp 1131cc engine. The new compression ratio is 6.1:1 instead of 5.8:1.
December 21, 1953	1-0575415	**Engine:** An oil bath cleaner is standard for all engines and models. V-belts are narrowed and the break-in instructions are deleted. The valve guides are now 55mm long, and the intake valve heads are 30mm in diameter. The pulley's thickness increased from 1.0mm to 1.25mm.
December 21, 1953	1-0575415	**Brakes:** The reservoir for the brake master cylinder is moved from the master cylinder to behind the spare tire.
December 21, 1953	1-0575415	**Heating:** The heat outlets are located in front and have protective grills.
December 21, 1953	1-0575415	**Electrical:** The 130-watt generator is replaced by a 160-watt model. The batteries are now fitted with a spring catch instead of a clamp with a spring. The same lock and depression is used for the doors and ignition.
December 21, 1953	—/—	**Interior:** The rear seat backrest is held down by rubber loops.

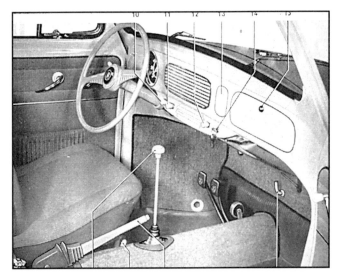

Part of a brochure was this image of the dashboard and an explanation of the various upgrades for the 1953 year.

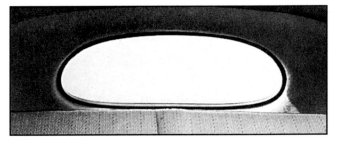

One pivotal moment in Volkswagen history happened on March 10, 1953, when the Oval Window officially replaced the split window. This added 23 percent more rearward viewing area than that of the previous Brezelfenster, pretzel-window.

1953

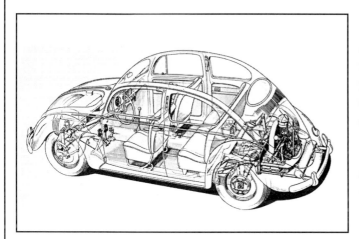

A detailed cutaway of the Oval Window Beetle in 1953.

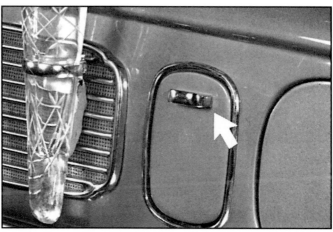

Showing consumers Volkswagen's attention to detail is this one small change in 1953, the small ashtray handle. Note the ornate bud vase.

To make fueling easier, the neck of the gas tank is virtually doubled, from 40 to 80mm.

All models now have an oil bath cleaner perched on the carburetor.

1954

Chassis Numbers:1-0579683 to 1-0781884
Engine Numbers: 700698 to 946526
Produced between January 1, 1954 and December 31, 1954

Engine horsepower was increased from 25 to 30bhp, beginning on December 21, 1953, and the top speed was raised to 68mph. This was achieved by raising the capacity of the engine from 1031cc to 1192cc and the compression ratio from 5.8 : 1 to 6.1 : 1. In addition, larger inlet valves (28 to 30mm) and exhaust ports were improved for better flow. The generator capacity was increased from 130 to 160 watts, and the carburetor is fitted with a vacuum take-off so that a vacuum advance distributor can be used on the higher performing engine.

The production average increased to 769 Beetles daily. The Standard VW cost only 3950 DM, and 900 DM more bought the Export Model. One of the first Volkswagen clubs met on the weekend of July 10–11 on the Killeburg in Stuttgart. 18,000 Volkswagen drivers came together as part of the second meeting of the Hunderttausender, which was open to any Volkswagen and owner that had achieved 100,000 kilometers on one engine. At that meeting, Heinrich Nordhoff announced: "We are still convinced that—I will say it over and over again, since again and again absolutely senseless and unfounded rumors arise of a new Volkswagen—that the blessing lies not in bolder and more magnificent new designs, but in the consistent and tireless redevelopment of every tiny detail until perfection is achieved, which is the mark of a truly astonishing car and which brings truly astonishing success."

Date	Chassis/Unit Numbers	Modification
January 25, 1954	1-0591433	**Engine**: The oil dipstick has a bent loop and cap.
February 5, 1954	1-0598459	**Brakes**: The plug seal diameter on the fluid reservoir for master cylinder enlarged to 17.85mm.
February 6, 1954	1-0598795	**Engine**: The oil cooler is now marked with the month and year of manufacture on bottom.
March 1, 1954	1-0607509	**Engine**: The flywheel seal is made with aluminum foil instead of paper.
March 2, 1954	1-0611493	**Fuel**: The tank filler cap is galvanized.
March 6, 1954	1-0613943	**Interior**: The door locks have a tighter rubber sleeves and are glued. Also, the locks are equipped with a longer rivet and a corrugated washer in between.
March 24, 1954	1-0623266	**Brakes**: The inside diameter of the front and rear brake hoses are 2.5mm, while the outside diameter decreases from 12.2mm to 10.0mm.
April 6, 1954	1-0631062	**Engine**: The oil pump housing is modified to clear the oil pump shaft.
April 21, 1954	1-0693872	**Electrical**: The distributor VJU 4BR 3 mk is equipped with improved springs for the centrifugal weights.
May 3, 1954	1-0645501	**Brakes:** The brake cylinders are mounted with two bolts instead of four.
May 6, 1954	1-0647384	**Brakes**: The rear backing plate has round holes instead of slots on the Standard Model.
May 7, 1954	1-0647704	**Brakes**: The rear backing plate has round holes instead of slots on the Export Model.
May 22, 1954	1-0656098	**Front Axle:** The torsion arms now have four lubrication grooves instead of three.

1954

May 25, 1954	1-0652823	**Interior, Convertible**: The rearview mirror has two sun visors. The passenger side has a grab handle, and two loop handles for the rear seat passengers.
May 28, 1954	1-0659075	**Engine**: The intake valve is made with a material that better resists heat.
May 1954	1-0660000	**Front Axle**: The front end has autogenously welded reinforcing plates instead of spot welding.
June 15, 1954	1-0668727	**Transmission**: The selector fork for the reverse sliding gear is forged instead of sheet metal.
June 25, 1954	1-0674360	**Engine**: The flywheel seal is made of 0.20–0.25mm paper instead of aluminum foil.
June 30, 1954	1-0676770	**Brakes**: The handbrake now has a rubber pad between push button and spring.
July 1, 1954	1-0678002	**Engine**: The cylinder head bore and filter plug is no longer required.
August 4, 1954	1-0689103	**Engine**: The thermostat has an elongated contact surface and opening in bracket.
August 10, 1954	1-0698300	**Interior**: The rear luggage compartment floor is no longer equipped with two holding rails.
August 31, 1954	1-0702742	**Engine**: The 77mm diameter piston now has a flat top and a compression ratio of 6.6:1.
August 31, 1954	1-0702742	**Engine:** The Solex 28 PCI carburetor's main jet is set at 117.5 and the correction jet is now 195.
August 31, 1954	1-0702742	**Engine**: The Solex 28 PCI carburetor now has a nylon float.
September 18, 1954	1-0716104	**Body**: The rear window is made of shatterproof glass for 8,000 cars.
October 1, 1954	1-0722916	**Engine**: The smaller pulley has a width of 20mm instead of 10.5mm.
October 13, 1954	1-0713718	**Engine**: The carburetor now has a plastic float.
October 18, 1954	1-0734000	**Electrical**: The stop light casing now has a drain hole at the bottom.
November 11, 1954	1-0751398	**Transmission**: The anti-vibration mounts are softer in front and harder in the rear for the Standard model.
November 12, 1954	1-0753096	**Engine**: The generator's fan wheel and small pulley are dynamically balanced.
December 10, 1954	1-0770501	**Body**: The door hinge now has an oil groove for pin lubrication instead of a hole.

1954

The 1954 Oval Window Beetle.

The new Beetle engine, with a 1200cc capacity. The vacuum advance is fitted to the distributor, and the center of the pre-heating pipe is a heating jacket for better heating the inlet manifold.

The top of the photo shows the larger windshield wiper arms, but the main focus is the option passenger grab handle.

The early '50s displayed some interesting patterns for the upholstery, something no enthusiast would scoff at today.

The heating inlet vents are now on the floor and through the defroster on the dashboard. The ignition lock is removed in place of an ignition lock/starter lock on the steering column. The dashboard light comes on when the outside lights are illuminated.

The brake master cylinder reservoir is now located behind the spare tire in the trunk.

1955

Chassis Numbers: 1-0781885 to1-01060929
Engine Numbers: 946527 to 1277347
Produced between January 1, 1955 and December 31, 1955

During the celebration ceremony for the one millionth Volkswagen, Nordhoff announced another price cut: 3790 DM for the Standard, 4700 DM for the Export and 5990 DM for the Cabriolet model. Because of this and improved production facilities and techniques, 279,986 Beetles were built in 1955, 87,520 more than the previous year. The Beetle was exported to over 100 countries, and 35,581 were sold in the U.S. alone.

Some notable changes were the enlarged brake light lenses, using twin filament bulbs, one for brake light and the other for taillight. The sound of the exhaust is improved with the addition of twin tailpipes. The exhaust pipes on the Export Model were chromed while the pipes on the Standard Model were painted black; for both models, the exhaust system was positioned 38mm higher to allow for increased clearance. For increased luggage space, the fuel tank was redesigned so that the uppermost part was smaller, allowing the fuel to flow down to the larger portion of the tank. In the interior, the steering wheel was changed to an easy-grip rim, and on the Export Model, the speedometer could be seen more easily because of the smaller steering wheel hub and deep-set spokes. The front seats were widened 30mm and are adjusted on slide rails. The backrests were now three-way adjustable on the Export Model. The window wings were redesigned to prevent break-ins, by securing the hooked-shape catch under a projection in the window channel, eliminating the possibility of lifting the window out of the channel. Inside, the operator would now push forward on the door handle to lock the door and pull back to open it.

Date	Chassis/Unit Numbers	Modification
January 4, 1955	1-0783227	**Engine**: The intake manifold is now treated with a special paint.
January 9, 1955	1-0787449-797357	**Front Axle**: The tie rods on approximately 1000 Standard Sedans are without grease points.
February, 8, 1955	1-0811212	**Front Axle**: Lifting cams are no longer provided on the Pitman arms.
March 5, 1955	1-0826740	**Chassis**: The choke cable is secured by a better sealing sleeve.
March 28, 1955	1-0848612	**Fuel**: The fuel pump now has two studs for better centering.
March 29, 1955	1-0848013	**Engine**: The camshaft slot width is now 5.6mm instead of 5.15mm.
April 1, 1955	1-0847967	**Electrical**: Flashing turn signals replaces indicator arms for USA, Canada and Guam.
April 1, 1955	1-0848900	**Engine**: The first oil change uses 10W year-round.
April 30, 1955	1-0870301	**Engine**: The ignition drive gear is now made of Aeterna bronze instead of steel.
May 3, 1955	1-0896851	**Body**: The engine lid springs are reinforced with a modified socket.
May 11, 1955	1-0881293	**Transmission**: The gearshift lever is now standard equipment on both standard and synchromesh transmissions.
May 31, 1955	—/—	**Chassis**: Frame numbers have been discontinued.
July 1955	1-0916456	**Transmission**: The ball bearing for the front pinion assembly now has a wider inner race.
July 11, 1955	—/—	**Engine**: The induction manifold of the 1192cc engineslight metal are marked with "30" on the light metal jacket to indicate a 30hp engine.
August 4, 1955	1-0929746	**Transmission**: The clutch spring plate setting is now 12 degrees (for merly 13 degrees).
August 4, 1955	1-0929746	**Exhaust**: All models now come with a single-chamber box with two

1955

Date	Chassis/Unit Numbers	Modification
		tailpipes and a connecting pipe for preheating tube.
August 4, 1955	1-0929746	**Interior**: The heat control knob is relocated to the front of the front seats instead of to the rear.
August 4, 1955	1-0929746	**Interior**: The front seats are 30mm wider. The front seats now have a three-way adjustable backrest for the Export Model only. The seat springs in the rear seats have changed along with a curved and thinner backrest. The number of lateral seat positions changes from two to seven. The front luggage compartment increases from 2.47cu.ft. to 3.0cu.ft. (a 20 percent gain), and the rear luggage space decreases from 4.59cu.ft. to 4.24cu.ft.
August 4, 1955	1-0929746	**Electrical**: The taillight housing is mounted 60mm higher.
August 4, 1955	1-0929746	**Body**: The sliding sunroof is now shorter with rounded corners, a plastic lining and plastic rollers (instead of leather). The bows decrease from two to one. The vent wing latch is curved instead of straight.
August 4, 1955	1-0929746	**Interior**: The locking hood release now is relocated further to the left.The cloth passenger loops give way to plastic, while the door and side panels now have leatherette stripes and moldings.
August 4, 1955	1-0929746	**Fuel**: The fuel tank shape is modified, while the filler diameter is reduced in size from 80mm to 60mm. The fuel tap is now without a filter and the switch is in a new location.
August 4, 1955	1-0929746	**Engine**: The generator pulley is secured with a 31mm bolt instead of a 36mm bolt, making the 36mm ring wrench obsolete and allowing the spark plug wrench to do double duty. Instead of the 175T1 spark plugs, all heads are fitted with 225T1 plugs.
August 4, 1955	1-0949746	**Brakes**: The hand brake cables that were attached to the brake rod are now attached to the hand brake lever.
August 4, 1955	1-0929746	**Steering**: The steering gear is limited by means of lateral stops at upper axle tubes, while the steering wheel is modified so that the spokes are positioned lower.
August 4, 1955	1-0948000	**Transmission**: The gearshift lever now has a spring-loaded steel locking ball.
September 29, 1955	1-0981275	**Suspension**: The shock absorbers, formerly TDZ 26 x 130, are now S 26 x 130.
October 14, 1955	1-0995357	**Engine**: Two of the crankcase bolts are 6 x 30.8G instead of 6 x 28.
November 6, 1955	1-1014694	**Rear Axle**: The Gleason 7:31 type V reduction gear is replaced with a 8:35 model.
December 19, 1955	1053294	**Interior**: The front seat runners have a transverse bracing and deeper grooves.

1955

In California, where this Beetle ended up, the Volkswagen was beginning to take off in popularity among the young and old alike.

In 1955, the steering wheel of the Export Model is redesigned so that it has an easier-to-grip wheel and deeper set spokes so the dashboard can be seen better.

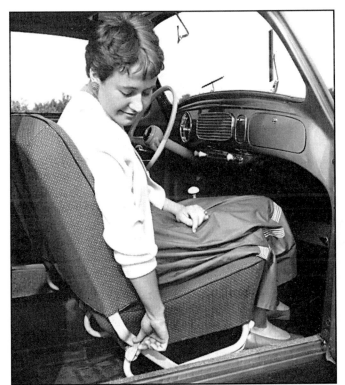

For comfort, the front seats are widened by 30mm and designed now for better comfort. The bottom of the seat is angled higher at the front and the backrest can be adjusted three ways.

The gear lever now has a twist to it to be better angled toward the driver. The door panels are topped with leatherette for less damage because of wear, and the door handles are now pulled back to open the door.

1956

Chassis Numbers: 1060930 to 1394119
Engine Numbers: 1277348 to 1678209
Produced between January 1, 1956 and December 31, 1956

Volkswagen did not make any major changes to the 1956 model. Most of the changes were minor. However, all Beetles were eventually fitted with tubeless tires, and the VW logo on the hubcaps are painted black instead of the matching color. An additional exterior mirror is fitted on the left side of the car for added viewing, and the oil intake pipe is shortened to keep the oil intake in the crankcase clear of sludge and water. Even though the combined workforce of the factory and offices grows to 35,672 employees and Volkswagen can boast 395,690 cars produced, the conflict in Suez reflects a negative effect on the exportation of cars, as the canal is a major avenue of ship transportation for Volkswagen.

Date	Chassis/Unit Numbers	Modification
January 14, 1956	1075548	**Interior**: The front seats are given additional support springs.
January 19, 1956	1092980	**Interior**: The lateral upholstery beading is more rounded on the front seat backrests.
January 23, 1956	1084218	**Steering**: A rubber washer is added to the base of the column.
January 27, 1956	1087746	**Engine**: The total length of the tapped insert for the spark plug decreases from 11.84mm to 11.34mm.
February 2 ,1956	1092980	**Interior**: The front seats backrests are equipped with a cardboard protection in the rear.
February 14, 1956	1109359	**Electrical**: The ground contacts are improved by galvanizing.
February 22, 1956	1113449	**Electrical**: The centrifugal force and vacuum curve in the top speed range are lowered by three degrees and five degrees.
February 24, 1956	1110980	**Body**: The outer door panel is reinforced near the vent window wing.
February 25, 1956	1117200	**Brakes**: The brake adjusting nut's total length decreases from 29.5mm to 21.0mm.
March 1956	—/—	**Body**: Ground clearance for the Export Model decreases from 170mm to 155mm.
March 7, 1956	1125652	**Brakes**: The adjusting hole is relocated.
April 3, 1956	1149147	**Body**: New colors are Prairie Beige, Coral Red, Horizon Blue and Diamond Green.
April 3, 1956	1149147	**Interior**: The horsehair mat inside the front seats is lengthened by 15mm in front.
April 16, 1956	1163469	**Transmission**: The hex head screw for the shift is decreased from 12mm to 6mm.
April 17, 1956	1165108	**Fuel**: The distance from the center of the tank to the center of the filler neck is reduced from 245mm to 215mm.
April 18, 1956	1167145	**Transmission**: The shift pin for fourth gear now has an eccentrical end instead of a cylindrical end.
April 25, 1956	1173160	**Body:** For one month only, the thickness of the metal for the hood is increased from 0.75mm to 0.80mm.
May 16, 1956	1191375	**Engine**: The bottom section of the oil induction pipe is shortened by 12mm.
May 22, 1956	1193483	**Transmission**: The Gleason reduction gear now has a tooth ratio of 7:31 instead of 8:35.

1956

Date	Chassis/Unit Numbers	Modification
May 25, 1956	1198184	**Engine:** The working surface of the 77mm cylinder is shorted by 8mm for 1000 engines.
June 5, 1956	1210230	**Engine:** The vacuum pipe, once above the choke cable, is now located under the throttle cable.
June 13, 1956	1216555	**Transmission:** The synchromesh reverse gear now has an annular inside groove with two oil holes (formerly one).
June 22, 1956	1227367	**Electrical:** The semaphores for the Inca Red Convertible are now yellow and a reddish shade (reddish shade to be discontinued August 14, 1956).
June 30, 1956	1232835	**Tires:** Eight hundred vehicles are fitted with tubeless tires.
July 1956	—/—	**Body:** The identification plates are modified on all models.
July 12, 1956	1243559	**Electrical:** The windshield wiper motor is now a permanent magnet type, made by SWF.
July 13, 1956	1248030	**Tires:** Tubeless tires (size 5.6 x 15) became standard equipment on the Export and Standard models.
August 6, 1956	1252386	**Body:** The color Agave is added to the line for the Export Sedan.
August 8, 1956	1257230	**Body:** The door locks now have adjustable striker plates.
August 14, 1956	1261493	**Engine:** The ignition coil is now a TE6 B1 instead of a TE6 A3, for improved ignition.
August 16, 1956	1259940	**Engine:** The length of the bore for the oil pump shaft is increased from 23mm to 25mm.
August 21, 1956	1266617	**Electrical:** 10,000 AVOG windshield wiper motors were fitted alternatively.
August 22, 1956	1270043	**Transmission:** The teeth on third and fourth gears are now offset by 180 degrees (except for three teeth), and the working sides are set back 0.2mm. All teeth are backed off two degrees.
August 31, 1956	1279013	**Front Axle:** The shock absorber is fitted with locking washers on the inside and outside instead of locking plates.
September 1956	—/—	**Fuel:** A rubber gasket is used around the fuel tank (in diameters 100mm, 80mm and 60mm) instead of cork.
September 4, 1956	—/—	**Body:** The colored VW emblem on the hub caps are now painted black only.
September 6, 1956	1283328	**Body:** The convertible top is fastened with brass pins and nails instead of iron pins and nails.
September 20, 1956	1307200	**Brakes:** The brake rod tube is shorted by 3mm.
September 27, 1956	1306289	**Engine:** The choke valve spring force is increased from 33g to 48g.
October 1, 1956	1307200	**Brakes:** The pedal clearance is improved.
October 10, 1956	1320179	**Steering:** The wheel is attached with a spline that has 48 teeth instead of 24.
October 19, 1956	1329017	**Body:** A rearview mirror is now standard equipment on all domestic-bound cars.
October 22, 1956	1329174	**Electrical:** The ground strap for the battery is now mounted to the floor plate instead of the body (convertible only). The strap is now 170mm long.
October 23, 1956	1326040	**Body:** The grease nipples are dropped from the door hinges on

October 23, 1956	1330627
October 25, 1956	1338160
December 1, 1956	—/—
December 1, 1956	1371001
December 10, 1956	1378864

all convertibles. Outside mirror is standard equipment.

Body: The cardboard sound dampeners in the engine compartment are made thicker.

Transmission: The Gleason ring gear tooth ratio is 7:31 (instead of 8:35).

Body: The colors Pearl Blue and Bamboo are added, while Iris Blue and Sepia Silver are dropped.

Body: There is now a rubber tube behind the rearview mirror (instead of a coil spring), and the glass is 3mm thick.

Transmission: The clutch pressure is reduced and the lining is made of Textar 50 S.

The 1956 Beetle with its new overriders on the bumpers, the bullet turn signals and tubeless tires.

The horsehair matting inside the front seats is now 15mm longer.

1957

Chassis Numbers: 1394120 to 1774680
Engine Numbers: 1678210 to 2156321
Produced between January 1, 1957 and December 31, 1957

The largest and most obvious change to the Beetle this year was the enlarged front window. By expanding the glass from the top and the sides, the window pillars were decreased in thickness, adding visibility. In addition, the rear window was enlarged as well. Inside, the control knobs and accessories have been redesigned and relocated: the glove box was enlarged, the pull ashtray was in the center of the dash for easy access for front occupants, and to decrease confusion. The distance between the lights and windshield wiper knobs have been increased. A piece of chromed trim runs the breath of the dashboard on the Export Model, and the side paneling material is synthetic. The roller ball accelerator was replaced by a flat pedal, and the deck lid was redesigned to easier hang the license plate. At the Auto Show in Frankfurt, Karmann presented its two-seater Ghia Cabriolet, with production beginning that August.

By November, the various plants in Germany employ 40,000 people, and the annual revenue tops two billion marks for the first time, with 52.5 percent of that money coming from the sales of the Export Model. The daily output (including Transporter production) reaches a phenomenal 2141 vehicles, with a total of 380,561 cars built.

In Australia, the Melbourne Volkswagen Pty Ltd is formed. The new subsidiary will manufacture Volkswagens using German-made VW parts.

Date	Chassis/Unit Numbers	Modification
January 9, 1957	1394163	**Heating**: The heating channels are in the side members and the hot air ducts in the front foot space are set back.
January 11, 1957	1408577	**Brakes**: The adjusting hole is now round instead of oval.
January 30, 1957	1428171	**Brakes**: The brake line between master brake cylinder and brake hose is galvanized with a dull finish instead of copper plated.
February 1, 1957	1429178	**Engine**: The thickness of the intake manifold wall is now 20 x 2mm instead of 18 x 1mm.
February 4, 1957	1430323	**Transmission**: The 2.4mm diameter oil bore in the fourth gear and pinion assembly is no longer required.
February 6, 1957	1430498	**Front Axle**: The left tie rod was 350mm and now is 354mm.
February 6, 1957	1436285	**Transmission**: The pinion locking plate tongue is now rounded instead of flat in a number of synchro transmissions.
February 12, 1957	1437984	**Transmission**: The shims for the second gear are 0.1mm and 0.15mm instead of 0.1mm and 0.2mm.
February 14, 1957	1444260	**Body**: The sliding roof cover increases in size from 1350mm to 1380mm.
March 1, 1957	1461126	**Body**: The window run channel is narrowed from 5.0mm to 3.5mm.
April 2, 1957	1499089	**Brakes**: The stop ring for the brake pedal shaft is 5mm wide instead of 10mm.
April 5, 1957	1498843	**Fuel**: The seal between the filter in the tank and the fuel tap is discontinued.
April 15, 1957	1510337	**Suspension**: The Boge shocks now have a high-pressure stage: 154kg (pull) and 48kg (push).
April 16, 1957	1509562	**Body**: The tube that holds the choke control cable increases in diameter from 8mm to 10mm.
April 24, 1957	1516457	**Interior**: The front and back seats are redesigned.

1957

Date	Chassis/Unit Numbers	Modification
April 24, 1957	1517414	Engine: The starter is now sealed off with a cover plate when not in operation.
April 29, 1957	1524059	Engine: The gaskets for the exhaust and heater pipe flange are changed from 1.4mm and 1.1mm to 1.5mm and 1.0mm respectively.
May 13, 1957	1536250	Engine: The oil cooler is now painted black and is now 226mm in height.
June 12, 1957	1569912	Engine: The dowel pin for the flywheel increased in length to 14mm by 0.3mm.
July 1, 1957	1584655	Transmission: The coast sides of the first gear teeth are offset 0.03–0.06mm.
July 2, 1957	1587862	Interior: The front seat has a quilted top padding with two retaining side clamps instead of the cotton wadding.
July 9, 1957	1597688	Body: The hole for the hood lock was 8.1mm in diameter and now is 6.5mm.
August 1, 1957	1600440	Fuel: There is now a plastic foam layer between the tank and luggage compartment. Formerly, it was cardboard.
August 1, 1957	1600440	Suspension: The internal splines of the torsion bars are shortened.
August 1, 1957	1600400	Body: The cool air vents are modified for better efficiency and improved water drainage. The rear deck lid receives an improved water seal, and the convertible lid's air intake slots are horizontal instead of vertical. The distance between the top of the license plate and the lamp is now 45mm, and the lamp uses a 5-watt bulb. Body: The windshield and rear window are enlarged. The throttle cable is 10cm longer, and the roller/lever is dropped, replaced by a rubber-covered pedal set 30mm further toward the front.
August 1, 1957	1600400	Electrical: The distance between the windshield wiper arms are reduced, and the blades are lengthened for a larger sweep area. The harness is laid in the left roof member (instead of the right), and there is a separate harness for generator and starter.
August 1, 1957	1600400	Brakes: The back plates are rotated 180 degrees so that the brake cylinder is in the top section instead of the bottom section on a few vehicles.
August 1, 1957	1600440	Steering: The bushing for the steering column tube is now made of plastic and is 50 percent smaller.
August 1, 1957	1600440	Fuel: The fuel consumption ratings show the Beetle is capable of an average of 32.2mpg, increased from 31.4mpg.
August 1, 1957	1601517	Transmission: The overall thickness of the clutch contact surface and collar has increased to 46.5mm by 0.5mm.
August 6, 1957	20-273650	General: The hub caps on the Panel Van and Single Cab are painted instead of chrome plated.
August 27, 1957	1631980	Transmission: The distance between the clutch cover contact surface at the flywheel and the release plate increased from 26mm to 27mm.
September 2, 1957	1641735	Engine: The carburetor's venturi is now made of plastic instead of metal.

1957

Date	Chassis/Unit Numbers	Modification
September 12, 1957	1657072	**Transmission**: The clutch linings are now Textar 50 S or 1533/9M. The thrust springs are reduced requiring less foot pressure at the pedal.
September 16, 1957	1649253	**Steering**: The steering wheel horn ring and hub for the Karmann Ghia coupe is lowered and the column is shortened.
September 16, 1957	1649253	**Body**: A 12mm-thick fiberglass mat is now between the firewall and the sound dampening cardboard on the Karmann Ghia coupe.
September 30, 1957	1669708	**Transmission**: The gasket for the gear shift housing to frame is made of elastic rubber with a domed rim instead of flat rubber.
October 1, 1957	1630550	**Fuel**: Instead of fitted separately, the gasket is glued directly to the fuel tap strainer.
October 1, 1957	1673351	**Brakes/Track**: The front brake shoes are now 40mm wide (with a 22.2mm cylinder) and arranged horizontally with two return springs. Brake backing plates are modified in shape, with wider drums and reinforcing ribs around periphery. The rear brakes cylinder is 19mm, and the backing plates are modified in shape. The bearing flange is turned deeper and the cap is shortened at the collar. The front track is 1305mm and the steering angle is 28/34 degrees.
October 18, 1957	1655524	**Engine**: The support and drilling in the fan housing discontinued, and the height of the cooler is 226.5mm. It is still painted black.
October 22, 1957	1699290	**Brakes**: The return springs for the brakes shoes are the same for front and back.
November 1, 1957	1709421	**Electrical**: The battery acid level is raised to the "acid level mark" or about 5mm above top edge of plates.
November 1, 1957	1713058	**Body**: The lock ring on the horn button is longer and wider.
November 6, 1957	1713583	**Body**: The battery mounting strap decreases in size from 468mm to 464mm.
November 11, 1957	1726006	**Transmission**: The roller bearing and ball bearing for the pinion and main driveshaft is changed to a needle bearing.
November 28, 1957	1747696	**Engine**: The exhaust valve guide is 60.0mm long, increased from 55.3mm.
December 1957	—/—	**Engine**: High-altitude jets are now offered.
December 2, 1957	1789961	**Body**: The spot welded stop is set 4mm further back.
December 19, 1957	1770158	**Electrical**: The Hella horn cover is now sealed with eight screws instead of six.

1957

For the 1958 model year, the windows are increased in size. The windshield is lengthened at the top and the sides by narrowing the A-pillar.

Out is the oval window and in is the era of the big-window Beetle. The rear window is 95 percent (almost twice as big) larger than the oval window.

The front window is increase by only 17 percent, but because of a larger rear window, it only makes sense to have a larger rear-view mirror. One of customers' major complaints had been solved.

The '57 Beetle got a completely new dashboard. The glove box was 50 percent wider and equipped with a spring-loaded button latch. Behind the grill to the left of the speedometer is a speaker for the optional radio. All of the control knobs are redesigned and placed further away from each other (to avoid confusion).The roller ball is gone and a flat pedal is used instead. On the Export and Convertible Models, a chrome stripe runs the length of the dash, and a rubber mat protects the floor.

If one were to cut the 1958 model year Beetle in half, like was done here, this is what it would look like. The purpose here is to show the increased window area and shape.

The front windows for the Beetle Convertible were only increased by eight percent for the front window and 45 percent in the rear. Note the horizontally organized rear louvers.

1958

Chassis Numbers: 1774681 to 2226206
Engine Numbers: 2156322 to 2721313
Produced between January 1, 1958, and December 31, 1958

In New York, Heinrich Nordhoff, Ferdinand Porsche and all of the Volkswagen employees were awarded the Elmer A. Sperry Prize. As part of his acceptance speech, Nordhoff stated: "I am far more attracted to the idea of offering people something of genuine value—a high-quality product with a low purchase price and an incomparable resale value—than to be continually pestered by a mob of hysterical stylists who try to sell people something they don't want to buy at all." Of the 1,495,256 automobiles produced in Germany in 1958, 37 percent of them were Volkswagens (or 553,399 Beetles).

Date	Chassis/Unit Numbers	Modification
January 3, 1958	1764743	**Body**: The U.S. models are now fitted with bumper guards on the front and rear.
January 7, 1958	1786160	**Body**: The disc wheels of the Convertible, Coupe and Ghia Convertible are painted pearl white.
January 9, 1958	1789807	**Fuel**: All VW Export Sedans are fitted with magnetic drain plugs.
January 15, 1958	1788180	**Body**: The defroster vent on the rear window now has a deflector (on the Ghia Convertibles).
January 20, 1958	1804134	**Body**: The rear glass run channels now have spring clips mounted in the top sections of the window frame instead of sheet metal tabs.
January 21, 1958	1805131	**Fuel:** The tank filler caps on approximately 30,000 vehicles have a modified ventilation system, so recognized by the "N" on the underside of the cap.
January 22, 1958	1802775	**Engine**: The Solex 28 PCI now has a 12mm-long spring for an idling screw.
February 10, 1958	1816990	**Interior**: The Beetle Convertible now has coat hooks.
February 10, 1958	1832100	**Steering**: A wax-dipped felt gasket is replaced by a rubber seal ring.
February 11, 1958	1833426	**Chassis**: The frame head, between the front axle support and under side of chassis is now fillet welded instead of butt welded.
February 18, 1958	1818035	**Body**: The Convertible windshield is increased in size.
March 20, 1958	1882550	**Tools**: The spark plug wrench now comes with a rubber sleeve instead of a holding spring.
March 24, 1958	1890983	**Engine**: The clutch driven plate features a spring cushion segment.
April 14, 1958	1904235	**Body**: Thirteen-millimeter hex bolts are used to secure the fenders to the body and the horn to the frame (formerly 14mm bolts).
April 29, 1958	1925488	**Steering**: The swivel (king) pin bush is now made of bronze and split down the middle.
May 8, 1958	1938979	**Steering**: The swivel (king) pin thrust washer is now made of plastic and is 3.15/3.05mm thick.
May 9, 1958	1943001	**Chassis**: The spring tension of the shift lever is now 4.5kg instead of 5.25kg.
June 5, 1958	1975105	**Engine**: The Solex 28 PCI carburetor now has a nylon venturi instead of one made from light metal.

1958

Date	Chassis/Unit Numbers	Modification
July 7, 1958	2013042	**Body**: The two rear deflector plates on the warm air outlets are omitted.
July 10, 1958	2003052	**Body**: The ashtray now has a PVC seal between it and the panel, which is cemented in place.
July 11, 1958	2020145	**Steering**: The steering gear mounting clamp is 3mm-thick sheet metal instead of 2.75mm thick. The torque for the nuts is 2.5–3.0mkg.
September 1958	—/—	**Engine**: Tropical fan belts are offered as a service part.
September 2, 1958	2071106	**Body**: The front hood lock can only be exchanged as a unit.
September 15, 1958	2084715	**Engine**: The bevel on the starter ring teeth (on the starter pinion engagement side) of the flywheel is omitted.
September 19, 1958	2086310	**Body**: The front hood lock operating cable is located closer to the steering column on the Karmann Cabriolet.
September 24, 1958	2100005	**Transmission**: The bonded rubber and metal transmission mounts are improved and identified with a "B" mark (formerly: "A").
October 14, 1958	2115600	**Chassis**: The end of the clutch cable tube is bell shaped instead of straight.
October 15, 1958	2120400	**Body**: A protective flannel cloth now covers the plastic rear window when the top is lowered on the KG Convertible.
October 31, 1958	2149710	**Body**: The outside rear view mirror is now enlarged with a modified mounting.
November 1, 1958	2149029	**Body**: The front hood now has a rear edge that is folded instead of a spot welded seam.
November 3, 1958	2154170	**Body**: The rear seat support is now part of the rear quarter panel instead of spot welded. The rear seat cushion support lengthened because of change.
November 3, 1958	2153001	**Electric**: The rotor and spark plug caps are remotely suppressed.
November 7, 1958	2163370	**Engine**: The exhaust valve guide is now 55.3mm by 0.6mm in dimension.
November 15, 1958	2168007	**Engine**: The rib underneath the spark plug bore on the cylinder head is strengthened by the addition of two cross fins on 50 percent of production.
November 18, 1958	2173883	**Chassis**: The eye for the pedal cluster bushing is reinforced.
November 28, 1958	2179586	**Suspension**: The eight-leaf torsion bars are no longer welded and are shortened by 7mm.
December 1958	—/—	**Engine**: The oil strainer is now permanently magnetized.
December 3, 1958	2193249	**Fuel**: The fuel pump now has a synthetic filter.
December 10, 1958	2207270	**Brakes**: The master cylinder is now secured with a hex bolt and spring washer instead of studs and nuts.

1959

Chassis Numbers: 2226207 to 2801613
Engine Numbers: 2721314 to 3424453
Produced between January 1, 1959, and September 31, 1959

The bodywork remained essentially the same, with most changes being technical. One exterior cosmetic change: push-button door handles and fixed mounts instead of a lever handle. Underneath, the engine and transaxle were tipped forward by two degrees to lower the pivot point of the swing axle by 15mm. Because of this, the rear suspension became more responsive and better at handling higher loads. The two-spoke steering wheel got the horn ring, a deeper hub and a self-canceling turn signal arm (with rubber stops for a quieter action). Above, the transparent sun visor was replaced by a color-matched cloth one. Underneath the rear seat, a kick panel is added for sound deadening, and inside, the battery gets a strap for easy removal. Production was increased by 25.9 percent, Volkswagen produces a total of 557,120 cars, and the company's revenue is over three billion marks. There were 54,120 employees working for Volkswagen this year, producing an average of 2,839 Volkswagens a day.

Date	Chassis/Unit Numbers	Modification
January 6, 1959	2232161	**Rear Axle:** The camber of the rear wheels decreases from four degrees to three degrees plus/minus 30 minutes.
January 12, 1959	2245160	**Tools:** The hubcap removal tool is included in the tool kit.
January 19, 1959	2252455	**Interior:** The sun visor on the Convertible is now padded instead of transparent plastic.
January 19, 1959	2256018	**Transmission:** The second gear drive pinion has 33 teeth instead of 32 teeth, while the main drive shaft gear is unaltered at 17 teeth.
January 22, 1959	2256907	**Front Axle:** The length of the left tie rod decreases in size from 814mm to 807mm, and the length of the right tie rod increases from 318mm to 325mm on right-hand-drive models only.
January 26, 1959	2261050	**Interior:** The grab handle for the front passenger is now flexible for the Convertible.
January 29, 1959	2269017	**Fuel:** The 80mm diameter filler cap is vented through a diaphragm instead of a Labyrinth-style venting.
March 10, 1959	2317671	**Interior:** The rear seat upholstery of the KG Convertible is raised and softer.
March 11, 1959	2331207	**Engine:** The top surface of the muffler is protected with zinc paint instead of black muffler paint.
March 23, 1959	2336743	**Body:** The door moldings are now secured by molding clips instead of molding pushed over screws.
March 31, 1959	2357120	**Heating:** The operating lever shafts of the heater junction box now have four flat surfaces.
April 6, 1959	2368910	**Electrical:** The heat range of the spark plugs are 175 instead of 225.
April 10, 1959	2369927	**Electrical:** To avoid jamming of the windshield wiper motor, the connecting rod now has a stop.
April 28, 1959	2395181	**Interior:** There is now a wider window lift channel for greater stability of window glass and guide channel on both KG models.
May 4, 1959	2409056	**Heating:** The heater junction box is now modified.
May 12, 1959	2422426	**Engine:** The fan now has a lock washer and modified nut.
May 13, 1959	2425182	**Engine:** The connections between the muffler and heater junction box muffler and tail pipe utilize conical asbestos seal rings and clamps.

1959

Date	Chassis/Unit Numbers	Modification
May 13, 1959	2428094	**Engine**: The muffler is now 10mm shorter.
May 19, 1959	2528668	**Engine**: The ratio of crankshaft pulley and fan drive is 1:1.75 instead of 1:2.
June 12, 1959	2477022	**Body**: The windshield wiper arm and blade are separate parts and interchangeable.
July 5, 1959	2503092	**Engine**: Tropical type fan belt is now standard equipment.
July 10, 1959	2503370	**Transmission**: The clutch pressure springs are stronger and painted gray.
August 6, 1959	2528668	**Front Axle**: A stabilizer bar is used on the front axle on the Deluxe and Convertible models.
August 6, 1959	2528668	**Body**: The outside door handles are redesigned for rigidity and push-button operated (formerly pull type). The headlight housing support is discontinued and the wires are now routed through rubber conduits. Sound deadening felt is added to the wheel housing and luggage compartment floor. On the KG models, the openings for the headlights are located 45mm (1.78inches) higher as well as further forward.
August 6, 1959	2528668	**Interior**: The passenger arm rest now has a recess area for gripping. The front seat backrest is contoured. The sun visor is now padded. The floor mats are a two-section design instead of a five-section design.
August 6, 1959	2528668	**Electrical**: The generator's wattage is increased from 160 to 180. The ignition lock is now 10mm deeper on the instrument panel. The taillight/stop light/turn signal were operated by the same bulb, but are now controlled by one bulb for each function. The dimmer switch is controlled by a push button on the indicator switch. The turn-signal switch is self-canceling. The horn ring is now a half ring. The windshield wipers only work when the ignition is on. The dimmer is protected by two fuses in the front fuse box. The indicator switch is fitted with sound deadening material.
August 6, 1959	2528668	**Heating**: The diameter of the front heating pipes increase from 32mm to 38mm.
August 6, 1959	2528668	**Steering**: A two-spoke type steering wheel with a recessed hub is now used.
August 6, 1959	2528668	**Engine**: The distance from the tip of the dipstick to the upper oil level mark is now 40mm instead of 44mm. The oil drain plug is now in the bottom plate of the oil strainer instead of the drain plug hole in case. Because of a two-degree incline during engine installation, the muffler tips were modified.
August 6, 1959	2528668	**Chassis**: The frame fork has a slight downward inclination toward the rear, and two studs are welded to the cross tube for front transmission mounting. A metal bracket is used for the kickboards.
August 6, 1959	2528890	**Engine**: The bore of the fan was 20mm in diameter and 160 watts, but is now 28mm and 180 watts.
August 6, 1959	2533000	**Engine**: The fan belts are now accompanied with 8–11 washers instead of 5–8.

1959

Date	Chassis/Unit Numbers	Modification
August 6, 1959	2533139	**Fuel:** The 28 PCI carburetor is modified with vacuum-advance-only distributor on all models.
August 29, 1959	2575175	**Body:** The vent-wing handle is stronger, and the inner triangular plate at the vent-wing handle has been strengthened.
October 1, 1959	2616684	**Electrical:** The speedometers on the Convertible models are lit with one light instead of two.
September 2, 1959	2582048	**Transmission:** A plastic boot is used for the shift lever instead of a rubber one.
October 7, 1959	2648938	**Front Axle:** The torsion arms on the link pin uses an 8mm hex hole in the face for easy adjusting.
November 5, 1959	2708099	**Fuel:** The fuel tap uses a cork seal instead of a Thiokol seal.
November 13, 1959	2725501	**Engine:** The valve stem is strengthened where it joins the valve head.
November 30, 1959	2765107	**Engine:** The outside diameter of the clutch cable increases from 6mm to 7mm.
December 18, 1959	2783954	**Body:** The window channel and weather strip is 100mm shorter.

The 1959 Beetle remained cosmetically unchanged since 1958, as more subtle changes were not readily visible.

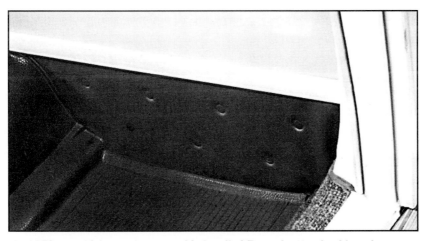

In 1959, rear kick panels were added, called Fersenbretter, heel boards.

1959

The passenger side added a footrest, and the front seats were angled back more and had a deeper curve.

The passenger armrests had an open area in the center to be used as a grip when closing the door.

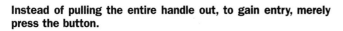

Instead of pulling the entire handle out, to gain entry, merely press the button.

In this production drawing of the underside of the pan, it shows the addition of an anti-roll bar to the front axle of all models.

1960

Model Year Chassis Numbers: 2801614 to 3192506 (to December 1960: 3551044)
Model Year Engine Numbers: 3424454 to 3912903 (to December 1960: 5428637)
1960 Model Year produced between October 1, 1959, and July 30, 1960

The Beetles produced in 1960 underwent the most drastic changes in recent years. Cosmetically, the semaphore turn signals were discontinued, and fender-mounted indicator lights were used. The rear lights were incorporated into the taillight housing. Most notably is the engine size. VW had not changed the engine output since 1954. For 1960, VW increased horsepower from 30 to 34bhp, much like they did the Transporter engine the year before. This increase was done by raising the compression ratio from 6.6 : 1 to 7.0 : 1. For breathing, a newly designed Solex 28 PICT carburetor was fitted with an automatic choke instead of the hand-operated one. To help the engine perform better while cold, inlet pipes were added to take heat from the engine and inject it from the left heat exchanger to the oil bath air filter. Transferring the power to the wheels is done through a fully synchromeshed four-speed transmission.

Amenities, such as a grab handle for passengers, a coat hook made of safer plastic, a standard-item sun visor for the front passenger and handles for the rear passengers, were also added. The speedometer was recalibrated to 140km/h, and absent are the red gear marks for first through third gears. The fuse box was relocated next to the steering column and accessible from inside the car. A windshield washer was added to all cars, and the reservoir was located in the trunk behind the spare tire.

Under the trunk lid, the fuel tank was redesigned again in the interest of better luggage space. The filler neck was moved to the left side of the car, and the tank has a flat appearance, with venting done at the neck instead of the cap. The brake fluid reservoir was fixed behind the spare tire by a strap.

Remarkably, Volkswagen produced 725,939 Beetles and 139,919 Transporters in 1960, nearly half of Germany's total car production for the year.

Date	Chassis/Unit Numbers	Modification
January 7, 1960	—/3351754	**Engine:** The valve clearance adjustment nut is now 13mm instead of 14mm.
January 12, 1960	2822646	**Brakes:** The protective hose is 120mm and secured to the cable with wire.
January 29, 1960	2855922	**Brakes:** The bolts on the front brake back plate are secured with a spring washer. The inner hub of brake drum is 2mm shorter.
February 2, 1960	2859237	**Body:** The diameter of the hood locking pin is decreased from 15mm to 8mm.
February 10, 1960	2882789	**Body:** The door handle lock cylinder is now chrome plated instead of zinc die cast on the convertible.
February 22, 1960	2907378	**Brakes:** A second brake cylinder manufacturer is used, identified by "S" on the cylinder. The first manufacturer's mark is "Ate."
February 25, 1960	2910843	**Front Axle:** The front wheel bearings are lubricated with lithium grease A-1060 instead of Universal grease A-052.
March 2, 1960	2921552	**Front Axle:** The torsion arm diameters are increased to 36.98mm and 37mm.
March 2, 1960	2921552	**Steering:** The steering damper is located between the upper axle tube and the long tie rod. The tie rods are now adjustable by two nuts and lock plate.
March 9, 1960	2943831	**Steering:** The sealing compound A-354 between the housing and the cover of the steering box is discontinued.
March 31, 1960	2983906	**Body:** The identification plate indicated that the permissible

1960

Date	Chassis/Unit Numbers	Modification
		maximum weight is 1120kg instead of 1110kg and the permissible rear axle load is 670kg instead of 660kg.
May 17, 1960	3083907	**Steering**: The steering damper is secured at the tie rod with two flat nuts and at the axle tube bracket with a lock plate.
May 25, 1960	3099936	**Fuel**: The fuel tap now has a Thiokol washer instead of cork.
June 7, 1960	3116871	**Rear Axle**: The torsion bars have depressions in the spring plate hub to prevent horizontal movement.
June 9, 1960	3135791/3849122	**Engine**: The edges to the flywheel's ventilation hole are better machined.
June 15, 1960	3149038	**Brakes**: The bracket for the front brake hose is moved 50mm to the rear and the brake line length is increased from 155mm to 170mm.
August 1, 1960	3192507	**Chassis**: The studs for the transmission mounting are discontinued and the transmission is now bolted to a support.
August 1, 1960	3192507	**Brakes**: The brake fluid reservoir is now made of translucent plastic instead of sheet metal.
August 1, 1960	3192507	**Transmission**: All forward gears are synchronized with the needle bearings and the main driveshaft is split.
August 1, 1960	3192507	**Suspension**: The rubber bumpers are lengthened by 10mm.
August 1, 1960	3192507	**Electrical**: All electrical cables have push-on connectors instead of being soldered to screws. The dimmer switch is moved 10mm to the left. The starter switch has a non-repeating lock. Semaphores are discontinued and instead flashing indicators are mounted on the front fenders.
August 1, 1960	3192507	**Interior**: All interior trim features match outside color. Added is a sun visor for the passenger as well as a grab handle.
August 1, 1960	3192507	**Transmission**: The ring gear is mounted with 17mm screws instead of 15mm screws and spring washers. The differential housing is no longer undercut.
August 1, 1960	3192507/5000001	**Engine**: The spark plug threads are cut into the head instead of using heli-coil inserts.
August 1, 1960	3192507	**Electrical**: The eight-point fuse box is located near the steering column instead of behind the instrument panel.
August 1, 1960	3192507	**Electrical**: The speedometer now reads 0 to 140k/h (0 to 90mph) without marks for speed limits per gear, and the protective tube for the cable is discontinued.
August 1, 1960	3192507/5000001	**Engine**: For arctic climates, the No. 1, 2, and 3 crankshaft bearings have steel backed shells added.
August 1, 1960	3192507/5000001	**Fuel**: The tank is modified, allowing for 4.94cu.ft. of truck space (formerly 3cu.ft.). Filler cap is moved to the left side of tank and increased to 87mm. The luggage compartment lining is lengthened accordingly.
August 1, 1960	3192507	**Body**: The door handles are modified. The key slot is horizontal with dust flap. Key profiles: SC, SU and SV.

1960

Date	Chassis/Unit Numbers	Modification
August 1, 1960	3192507	**Body**: The rear apron and deck lid are lengthened to accommodate longer engine.
August 1, 1960	3192507	**Interior**: The seat designs are improved for more springs and padding.
August 1, 1960	3192507/5000001	**Fuel**: The 28 PCI carburetor is replaced by a 28 PICT model.
August 1, 1960	3192507/5000001	**Engine**: The compression ratio was changed from 6.6:1 to 7.0:1, increasing the engine's power from 30hp to 34hp.
August 1, 1960	3200001/5016001	**Engine**: The generator pulley disc thickness is increased from 2mm to 2.5mm.
August 1, 1960	3195309/5016085	**Engine**: The camshaft thrust bearings now have annular oil grooves.
August 1, 1960	3197504/5022942	**Engine**: The cap for the oil filter is given a softer spring.
August 5, 1960	3223145/5042363	**Heating**: The preheater tube is given a new gasket and the internal diameter decreases from 16mm to 6mm.
August 12, 1960	3233148	**General**: The year of manufacture is not marked on the identification plate.
August 19, 1960	3248025	**Electrical**: The timing is retarded from 7.5 degrees before TDC to 10 degrees before TDC
September 21, 1960	3315740/5096200	**Engine**: The dipstick is modified.
October 3, 1960	3335848	**Suspension**: The Boge front shock absorbers are now approximately 26 percent softer.
October 3, 1960	3335848	**Suspension**: The Fichtel & Sachs rear shock absorbers are now approximately 35 percent softer.
October 10, 1960	3361751	**Body**: The hood lock pin guide is lengthened 5mm and provided with a curved collar.
October 13, 1960	3373369/5222819	**Fuel**: The hose between the fuel pump and the carburetor is now made of braided rubber.
October 20, 1960	3390251	**Electrical**: The resister type ignition cables are now orange-red and dark red.
October 31, 1960	3396921	**Steering**: The Stabilus and Hemscheidt model steering dampers are replaced by a Boge model.
October 31, 1960	3405001	**Interior**: The accelerator pedal is mounted higher and has a longer rubber cover.
November 9, 1960	3433280	**Fuel**: The accelerator tube runs through a synthetic tube between the frame and the engine.
November 8, 1960	3432861/5282381	**Engine**: The blades of the cooling fan increase in number from 16 to 28 blades.
November 24, 1960	3465332/5326955	**Engine**: The No. 4 crankshaft bearing now has an annular oil groove and oil drain groove.
December 12, 1960	3511065	**Brakes**: The reservoir and the master cylinder are connected by a flexible hose.

1960

The 1960 VW underwent significant changes, the most in recent years.

By redesigning the fuel tank, luggage space inside the trunk was increased by 60 percent as show in this cross section.

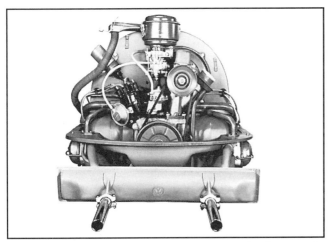

The choke cable was omitted in the 1960 production year. In its place is the new automatic choke Solex 28PICT carburetor.

The air cleaner now is fitted with an intake air preheater (black tube) to improve idling and low engine speeds.

For the Export Model dashboard, a grab handle is added, as well as a padded sun visor for the passenger.

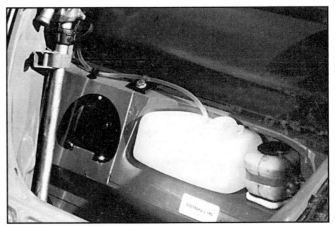

Behind the spare tire is a new transparent brake fluid reservoir as well as a one-liter windshield washer bottle.

1961

Model Year Chassis Numbers: 3192507 to 4020589 (to December 1961: 4400051)
Model Year 1200cc Engine Numbers: 3927803 to 3924023 (to December 1961: 3931468)
Model Year 1300cc Engine Numbers: 5000000 to 5958948 (to December 1961: 6375945)
1961 Model Year produced between August 1, 1960, and July 31, 1961

A two-section designed taillight housing allowed the rear turn signals to be more visible while the lights were on at night. Other changes: the front hood lid was spring loaded, the windshield washer was switched to pneumatic instead of hand operated (and the compressed air could be changed/replenished at any service station). The addition of a fuel gauge replaced the need or use of a reserve valve, and a change in the setting knob allowed the front seats a great range of adjustment. On the face of the speedometer, a red line indicates the 50km/h mark on domestic models.

Date	Chassis/Unit Numbers	Modification
January 2, 1961	3550952	**Body**: The VW emblem is secured by three grooved pins and plastic retainers instead of four hooks and a sealing compound.
January 16, 1961	3597114	**Transmission**: The Saxomat gear shift lever uses a stronger pressure spring.
January 19, 1961	3606032	**Fuel**: The delivery pipe was angled upward and the gasket between the filter and the pump cover is modified accordingly.
January 20, 1961	3607316	**Brakes**: The sharp edges on the frame surrounding the front brake cables are now folded back.
January 30, 1961	3621636	**Body**: There are now seals in the corners of the cowl panel under the front hood.
February 1, 1961	3627442	**Engine**: The fan pulleys now have a ratio of 1.75 : 1 instead of 1.8 : 1.
February 14, 1961	3672005	**Electrical**: The rubber caps for the ignition leads are discontinued on the ignition coil.
February 17, 1961	3681132	**Engine**: The hex nuts on the exhaust clips' fixing screws are replaced with self-locking nuts.
March 20, 1961	3752922	**Engine**: The first filling oil capacity is increased from 1.5L to 1.75L.
March 25, 1961	3712664	**Body**: The lip on the weather strip around the door striker plate is approximately 4mm wider.
March 28, 1961	3771255	**Interior**: The backrests of the front seats are secured with bolt and a cap nut.
March 29, 1961	3771982	**Suspension**: The Fichtel & Sachs offers a 26 percent softer version of shock absorber.
April 11, 1961	3806249	**Engine**: There is now a connecting hose between the oil bath air cleaner and the oil filler instead of a breather tube.
May 2, 1961	3856472	**Electrical**: The rear stop light and turn signal light are compartmentalized.
May 4, 1961	3862145	**Interior**: The speedometer has a red line on the scale for the 50km marking (only speedometers in kilometers).
May 4, 1961	3862489	**Body**: The front hood seal becomes one piece.
May 6, 1961	3866883	**Engine**: The stop for the throttle ring is 8–9mm thick rubber instead of flat.
May 10, 1961	3874581	**Engine**: The exhaust valves are of a modified material instead of chrome 193.

1961

Date	Chassis/Unit Numbers	Modification
May 25, 1961	3912101	**Front Axle**: The number was stamped in the torsion arm stop, but now is in white on the right anchor plate above the top torsion arm. The letter denoting production date is also stamped on right torsion arm stop.
May 31, 1961	3915597	**Engine**: The wall thickness of the exhaust pipe for cylinders No. 1 and 3 have increased from 1.5mm to 2.0mm.
June 13, 1961	3960131	**Electrical**: Instead of various colors of red, the ignition cables are now only the blue version.
June 16, 1961	3959952	**Engine**: The pushrod seals are uniformly white plastic instead of red and green rubber.
June 30, 1961	3933263	**Steering**: The worm and sector style steering is replaced by the roller type for Germany and Export convertible models.
June 30, 1961	3933263	**Body**: Anthracite and Pacific Blue paint codes are added to the palette, while Paste Blue is discontinued.
JulJuly 31, 1961	4010995	**Fuel**: Replacing the fuel tap, a fuel gauge is added for the Deluxe and Convertible models.
July 31, 1961	4010995	**Heating**: Vents are added in the front foot well with sliding covers (except for the Standard model).
July 31, 1961	4010995	**Heating**: Under the rear seats, warm air vents are added in the kickboards (Deluxe only).
July 31, 1961	4010995	**Interior**: The front seat runners are lengthened toward the rear (for taller front passengers) from 100mm to 120mm (except on the Standard Model).
July 31, 1961	4010995	**Frame**: The travel and leverage of the clutch pedal is increased by lengthening the clutch pedal shaft by 1.4mm (except on Standard Model)/
July 31, 1961	4010995	**Steering**: The worm and sector style steering is replaced by the roller type for Deluxe models, Germany only.
July 31, 1961	4010995	**Body**: The front hood is supported by two spring-loaded supports.
July 31, 1961	4010995	**Interior**: The ignition switch now has a steering lock.
July 31, 1961	4010995	**Electrical**: The ignition has to be on in order for the horn to work. The windshield wiper is assisted by a pneumatic system. Press button on the wiper switch to activate the wiper fluid. The speedometer now has a green indicator warning light (instead of red) in addition to starting at 15mph (10km).
July 31, 1961	4057923	**Interior**: The front seat backrests adjust further backward and forward because of a better cam design.
August 2, 1961	4011959	**Engine**: The heater junction boxes are held together with metal lugs on the front half of the box instead of tapping screws.
August 2, 1961	4027181	**Interior**: The pedal cluster is now maintenance free (except for Standard Model).
August 2, 1961	4036536	**Brakes**: The bearing for the main cylinder operating rod (connected to the foot pedal) is lowered 5mm for more power.

1961

Date	Chassis/Unit Numbers	Modification
August 8, 1961	4036536	**Brakes**: The hand brake cable now has a protective sleeve, and the unit is maintenance free without the use of grease nipples.
August 30, 1961	4089142	**Front Axle**: The left and right tie rods are adjustable and maintenance free, instead of only the right tie rod being adjustable and the whole unit requiring grease.
September 1, 1961	4090312	**Steering**: The lock nut for the adjustment screw of the steering worm now torqued to 2.5mkg.
September 16, 1961	4090760	**Transmission**: The slot for the axle shaft on the side gear increased from 22.5 + 0.5mm to 24.5 + 0.5mm.
October 2, 1961	4165118	**Engine**: The junction between the plate and hub is reinforced and the gland nut collar is lengthened by 1mm.
October 2, 1961	4163317	**Engine**: The exhaust valves are now flatter.
October 13, 1961	4205477	**Engine**: The preheater pipe of the intake manifold is 20 x 2.5mm increased from 20 x 2.0mm.
November 1, 1961	4236757	**Steering**: The worm and sector style steering is replaced by the roller type for Export Deluxe models.
November 1, 1961	4244394	**Engine:** The paper gasket around the flywheel and crankcase is replaced with a sheet metal gasket, and the sealing surface has a slightly conical inward shape.
November 16, 1961	4289952	**Interior**: The gear shift lever is now conical with a smaller knob.
November 17, 1961	4290738	**Transmission**: The two ribs on the throat of the gearshift housing are lengthened.
November 21, 1961	4299743	**Engine**: The oil filler gland nut collar increases its height from 3.8-0.5mm to 5-0.5mm.
December 5, 1961	4325735	**Transmission**: The rubber bush for the spring plates are now excentricly shaped instead of concentric.
December 5, 1961	4327475	**Engine**: There are now oil drillings on the reverse side of the crankshaft.
DDecember 14, 1961	4357893	**Body:** The phosphated door hinges are now treated with molybdenum disulphide instead of oil.

1961

Over 43 improvements made the 1961 model Beetle better than ever.

So the turn signal lights could be better seen when the driving lights were on, the housing was switched to a dual section. Shown here is the European setup with the amber turn signal lenses.

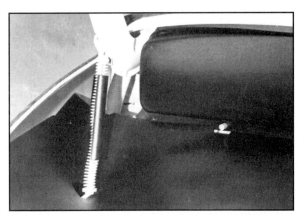

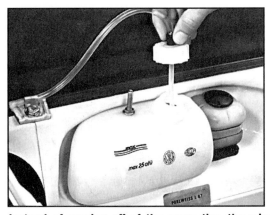

The trunk hood is now supported by springs instead of the locking support arm (that was often forgotten about when the owner tried to close the trunk and ended up damaging the panel).

Instead of running off of the spare tire, the windshield wiper fluid was automated via a compressed air tank.

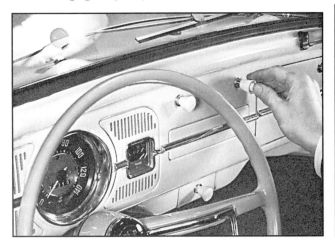

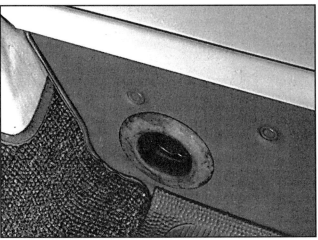

The windshield wiper switch was redesigned to accommodate the pneumatic washer.

Air outlets were added in the heel boards.

1961

The heating outlets in the front floorboards were now equipped with sliding covers to adjust the air flow.

Advanced for its time, and well ahead of the law, seatbelt anchor points were added for the addition of optional seatbelts.

The seat rails were adjusted further to the rear, so that tall passengers could be more comfortable. As well, backrests could be adjusted further to the rear also.

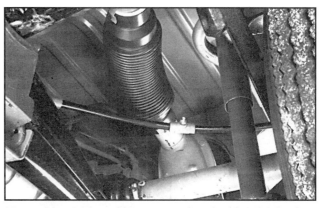

The parking brake cable came equipped with a lubrication nipple until August 1961. For the 1962 model, the parking brake cable was maintenance free.

The upholstery design for 1962 became more and more fashionable with the times.

The starter/ignition lock mounted on the steering column is standard for all models. A fuel gauge is added as well.

1962

Model Year Chassis Numbers: 4010995 to 4846835 (to December 1962: 5225042)
Model Year 1200cc Engine Numbers: 3924024 to 3942914 (to December 1962: 3949823)
Model Year 1300cc Engine Numbers: 5958948 to 6935203 (to December 1962: 7373000)
1962 Model Year produced between August 1, 1961, and July 31, 1962

The introduction of heat exhangers offered the passengers and driver fresh heated air instead of merely air passed over the cylinders and directed into the car. Gone are the cable brakes, replaced by hydraulic brakes fitted on all models. On the hood, all Wolfsburg crests were removed and replaced with a newly designed VW logo. The chrome trim was lengthened to fit.

A cleanable plastic/vinyl headliner was installed, replacing the woolen one previously used. The 1962 Beetles really only had small improvements, but no major changes.

Date	Chassis/Unit Numbers	Modification
January 5, 1962	4388450	**Rear Axle**: The inner spacer ring thickness of the rear wheel bearings increase from 5.9–6.1mm to 6.45–6.65mm.
January 8, 1962	4391365	**Interior:** The luggage compartment lining and wire cover are now tempered cardboard.
January 16, 1962	4420885	**Body**: The rubber seals for the glass and window regulator channel lengthened to better drain water.
January 29, 1962	4464038	**Clutch**: The clutch pressure is increased from 300–325kg. to 315–340kg. and the clutch cover is now marked with a "B".
January 15, 1962	4432260	**Fuel**: The fuel pump's rocker arm is now a pressed part (one piece) instead of a two-piece cast part.
February 5, 1962	4463485	**Electrical**: The speedometer cable is now inside a metal casing with a plastic sheathing instead of a plastic tube.
February 6, 1962	4477631	**Transmission**: The rubber transmission mounts have an increased shore hardness from 53 in the front and 65 in the rear to 60 in the front and 70 in the rear.
February 24, 1962	4519277	**Engine**: The crankcase is ventilated by a breather pipe connected to the reservoir on the underside of the oil bath air cleaner instead of on the oil bath air intake.
March 1, 1962	4528768	**Fuel**: The ventilation tube for the fuel tank is now made of rubber with a protective coating instead of polyurethane.
March 14, 1962	4570540	**Engine**: The outer surfaces of the intake manifold and preheater pipes are treated with a zinc paint instead of a phosphate.
March 19, 1962	4581537	**Transmission**: The gearshift lever is now spring loaded with a sliding round-headed bolt instead of with a soldered-in guide with a spring and ball.
March 26, 1962	—/—	**Body**: The 1500 model now offers a steel sliding sunroof.
April 2, 1962	4609565	**Engine**: The flange for the carburetor on the intake manifold is increased from 5.5mm to 7mm.
April 5, 1962	4630938	**Brakes**: The brake system is changed from hydraulic to mechanical.
April 5, 1962	4630938	**Chassis**: The track width of the Standard Model is now 1305mm in front instead of 1290mm, allowing the smallest turning radius of 11.0 meters instead of 11.5 meters.
April 9, 1962	4636869	**Fuel**: The fuel line between the carburetor and the fuel pump is now a

1962

Date	Chassis/Unit Numbers	Modification
		pipe with flexible endings instead of a braided rubber hose.
April 17, 1962	4659008	**Clutch:** A Jurid or Beral lining is used on the flywheel side of the 180mm clutch plate and Textar on the pressure plate side.
April 18, 1962	4583679	**Fuel:** The diameter of the fuel pump push rod is decreased from 7.9mm to 7.83mm.
April 19, 1962	4661868	**Engine:** The diameter of the oil drain passage is doubled in size from 3mm to 6mm.
April 28, 1962	4671926	**Body:** The number of screws on the door hinges is decreased from four to three.
April 28, 1962	4672922	**Body:** The window regulators are now fitted with springs.
May 3, 1962	4683160	**Clutch:** All of the pressure springs are colored brown instead of three yellow and three gray-blue.
May 16, 1962	4723425	**Heater:** The plastic support cage in the rear hose is replaced by a wire mesh hose with two asbestos rings.
May 28, 1962	4745703	**Engine:** The first filling of oil increases from 1.75L to 2.5L of oil.
May 28, 1962	4747856	**Engine:** The oil used was changed from SAE 10 to SAE 20.
June 1, 1962	4706884	**Interior:** The pedal cluster now requires a lithium grease.
June 13, 1962	4793801	**Body:** The screws for the door striker plate are no longer countersunk.
July 30, 1962	4846836	**Engine:** The oil cooler now has a perforated plate.
July 30, 1962	4764157	**Body:** The rear window of the convertible is increased 30 percent.
July 30, 1962	4846836	**Interior:** The insulation of the floor plates is now done with thicker Bitumen insulation.
July 30, 1962	4764158	**Body:** The Karmann Ghia Cabriolet now displays the spelled out "Volkswagen" lettering.
August 1, 1962	4847723	**Front Axle:** The shock absorber is now mounted using a M12 x 1.5 hex instead of a threaded bushing through the anchor plate.
August 1, 1962	4868581	**Engine:** Formerly two parts, the cam follower is now a one-piece cast with a pressed-in ball socket. The head is 3.9mm thick.
August 2, 1962	4847970	**Transmission:** The case's clearance is modified for a 200mm diameter clutch.
August 2, 1962	4874267	**Engine:** The walls of intake and preheating pipe increased in thickness from 1.2mm to 2.8mm, and instead of black paint, the pipes are sprayed with A211 zinc calcium. The oil fumes are now directed into the oil bath air cleaner instead of released into open air.
September 3, 1962	4937241	**Engine:** The distributor drive pinion is now fitted with two 0.6mm-thick washers instead of one 1.25mm-thick washer.
September 18, 1962	4978442	**Brakes:** The reservoir for the brake fluid now has a screw top instead of a stopper.
September 21, 1962	4988623	**Engine:** The depth of the two upper piston ring grooves is reduced by 0.6mm, and the new piston rings have a chamfer on the inner rim.

1962

Date	Chassis/Unit Numbers	Modification
October 1, 1962	5010448	**Body**: The Wolfsburg coat of arms is discontinued and the VW emblem is added to the front hood. The molding is extended.
October 3, 1962	5015376	**Steering**: The steering gear is now lubricated using SAE 90 gear oil instead of SAE 90 hypoid gear oil.
November 2, 1962	5007275	**Transmission**: The ribs on the gearshift housing are lengthened.
November 2, 1962	5094272	**Electrical**: The gear change markings on the speedometer are done in mph instead of kmh.
November 9, 1962	5120731	**Frame**: The guide for the clutch cable is moved 2mm toward the center of the car.
December 15, 1962	5199980	**Heating**: The fresh air is now heated in heat exchangers instead of heated by the cylinders.
December 15, 1962	5199980	**Electrical**: The spark plug connectors now have plastic caps.
December 15, 1962	5199980	**Heating**: The heater pipe between the heater muffler and the body is now insulated with a plastic tube.

For the 1962 production year, a host of details are improved. For example, the Wolfsburg crest is removed from the front hood, and as a result, the hood trim is lengthened.

The Beetle now enjoyed a steadily rising increase of improvements year after year. For the 1962 Model year, at least 25 mechanical and cosmetic changes were made.

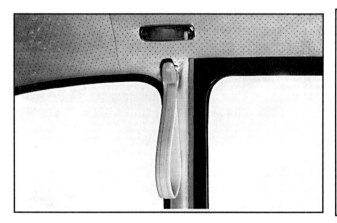

Instead of cloth, the headliner is made of a plastic-vinyl material.

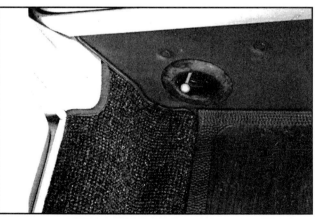

In the Export Model, heat regulating levers are within the air outlets on the heel boards.

1963

Model Year Chassis Numbers: 4846836 to 5677119 (to December 1963: 6016120)
Model Year 1200cc Engine Numbers: 3942915 to 3959303 (to December 1963: 3965218)
Model Year 1300cc Engine Numbers: 6935204 to 7893118 (to December 1963: 8264628)
1963 Model Year produced between July 30, 1962, and July 31, 1963

Though it was still available on the Standard Model until August 1967, the folding sunroof on the Export Model was discontinued. Instead, a steel, sliding sunroof was used. On the back, a newly designed license plate light (with bulbs and sockets borrowed from the Type III) was added to the deck lid for better visibility. In November 1963, broader turn signals are used, and their position on the front fenders is different. The steering wheel's semicircular horn ring is removed and thumb buttons are used instead, while the accent in black VW logos on the hub caps is discontinued.

In 1963, Volkswagen steps ahead of all German manufacturers when it reaches 6.84 billion marks in sales, making it the biggest company in Germany. They enjoyed a 42.4 percent share in all auto sales domestically, manufacturing 1,029,591 cars. With 685,769 cars exported, VW becomes the largest automobile exporter in the world. Daily production reaches 5,229 cars on the newly started fully automatic production line.

Date	Chassis/Unit Numbers	Modification
January 8, 1963	5225301	**Clutch:** The cable hook for the clutch pedal shaft is inclined a further three degrees backward.
January 24, 1963	5261830	**Clutch:** The clutch cable of the Export Model is now 10mm shorter.
January 28, 1963	5264811	**Body:** The door hinges are now lubricated with acid-free oil.
January 30, 1963	5271918	**Engine:** The exhaust valve head angle is decreased from 46 degrees to 45 degrees.
February 1, 1963	—/—	**Body:** Gulf Blue introduced.
March 6, 1963	5348759	**Tools:** Instead of two screwdrivers, included in the tool box is one with two blades.
March 12, 1963	5357922	**Rear Axle:** The diameter of the mounting point for the rear axle retainer is 131mm, decreased from 134mm.
April 1, 1963	5419871	**Body:** The seals for the bumper brackets are now made from a synthetic material instead of rubber.
April 3, 1963	5440221	**Interior:** The contact surfaces of the adjustment cam for the front seat backrests are enlarged.
April 24, 1963	5479829	**Interior:** The headliner is now supported by tensioning wire with plastic caps instead of rubber tubing.
April 29, 1963	5488894	**Interior:** The sliding sunroof now has one-piece runners instead of divided runners.
May 15, 1963	5540290	**Transmission:** The internal rib on the gearshift housing is removed, and the lower web of the breathing compartment is modified.
June 1, 1963	5578122	**Fuel:** The amount of fuel injected from the 28 PICT carburetor per stroke is increased from 1.1cc to 1.4cc.
July 4, 1963	5652156	**Interior:** The knob for the hood locking cable is moved 10mm toward the outside of the Convertible model.
July 4, 1963	5661082	**Transmission:** The clutch is fitted with heat-resistant pressure springs on the Export Model engine number 7860588.
August 5, 1963	5677119	**Steering:** The semicircle horn ring is discontinued. In its place are twin thumb buttons.

1963

Date	Chassis/Unit Numbers	Modification
August 5, 1963	5677119	**Interior:** All operating knobs and the steering wheel are colored silver beige instead of black.
August 5, 1963	5677119	**Interior:** The seats and headliner are now made of plastic vinyl insteadof cloth. The headliner is one piece.
August 5, 1963	5677119	**Interior:** Instead of beading and oiled paper on the door trim panel, a seal is added between the door inner panel and the trim panel.
August 5, 1963	5677119	**Body:** The license plate mounting holes are repositioned. Sea Blue, Anthracite, Pearl White, Ruby Red, Panama Beige, Java Green and Bahama Blue are introduced. The VW emblem on the wheel covers are no longer in color. The 1200 Sedan features a sliding metal sun roof instead of a folding sunroof.
August 5, 1963	5677119	**Tires:** The tire pressure is increased from 23psi to 24psi.
August 15, 1963	5699145	**Body:** The door check rod is now bent at a 90 degree angle at the rubber buffer end.
September 3, 1963	5749573	**Transmission:** All Type I models are now fitted with Type II shift lever stop plates.
September 10, 1963	5765471	**Front Axle:** The Hoesch shock absorbers have a single tube with plastic protective sleeves. The piston pulls in a downward direction.
October 1, 1963	5815778	**Engine:** The condensation drain pipe (for crankcase ventilation) is fitted with a rubber valve.
October 11, 1963	5834782	**Body:** The seals around the door locks are strengthened by 20mm.
October 28, 1963	5875847	**Frame:** The opening for the gearshift rod coupling is enlarged.
October 31, 1963	5888135	**Body:** The holes in the front fenders and side panels are altered due to the relocation of turn signals.
October 31, 1963	5888135	**Body:** The license plate housing is widened for the U.S. models (this change was made on August 5, 1963, with 5677119 for the Germany market).
October 31, 1963	5888135	**Body:** The turn signals are modified.
November 12, 1963	5909656	**Engine:** Because of the enlarged automatic choke, there is now a depression on the lower part of the filter for the oil bath air cleaner.
December 19, 1963	6009512	**Engine:** The rocker arm mechanism is modified on the export model. The inclination of the valves is increased and the rocker shaft is repositioned.

Imports of the Volkswagen for 1963 increased by almost 44,000 compared to the year before, as 277,008 were brought into the country.

1964

Model Year Chassis Numbers: 5677119 to 6502399 (to December 1964: 115410000)
Model Year 1200cc Engine Numbers: 3959304 to 3972440 (to December 1964: 3984729)
Model Year 1300cc Engine Numbers: 7893119 to 8796622 (to December 1964: 9339890)
1964 Model Year produced between August 1, 1963, and July 31, 1964

The front window is increased in size by a remarkable 28mm upward, giving the driver a broader view of the road. As well, the A and C pillars are more narrow, allowing the rear window to increase in size 20mm higher and 10mm wider. Door windows and front vent windows are enlarged, and the chrome pillar between the vent window and the door window is no longer vertical but slanted. The single arm window raiser is replaced by a cable operation, and the locking handle of the vent window no longer has a push button release, allowing easier operation.

In the rear, the T handle to open the deck lid is replaced by a push button latch made of high-grade chrome, and the catch automatically latches when lowered.

Inside, the rear seat can be folded down and secured with a strap, the sun visors can be swiveled to the sides, and the windshield wiper is lengthened by 15mm because of the increased window size. The park position of the wiper blades for the Export Model and the Cabriolet is on the left. Two swivel levers allow the driver to operate the heat more quickly: the right lever (red knob) operates the heat, while the left lever (white knob) controls the opening and closing of the flaps of the rear footwell heating.

Volkswagen invests 154.4 million marks in the new plant in Emden and expands the plant in Port Elizabeth, South Africa. Volkswagen loses their suit with the former VW Savers in March. Each of the 89,000 Savers are given an up to 600 mark discount on a VW 1200 or 100 marks in cash. 18,000 Beetles are delivered to the Savers and 41,000 compensation payments are given out.

Costing 150 million marks a year, 68 specially designed ships are chartered to carry 470,000 Beetles to countries around the world, but mostly to the United States.

Date	Chassis/Unit Numbers	Modification
January 17, 1964	6041854	**Body**: All vehicles are undercoated with a wax-based seal.
February 4, 1964	6093564	**Engine**: The diameter of the number one bearing journal of the crankshaft on the Export Model is reduced by 0.005mm to allow for more play.
February 7, 1964	6105201	**Engine**: The 2.5mm drilling for the throttle ring is now plugged with a rubber ball on the Export Model.
February 24, 1964	6147942	**Steering**: The radius of the steering worm stop in the steering gear housing is decreased from 3mm to 2.5mm. The housing now has a distinguishing "Mark 74" cast in.
March 16, 1964	6212132	**Engine**: The top vacuum drilling in the lower part of the carburetor is closed and equipped with a Cyclone filter.
March 17, 1964	6213182	**Transmission**: The radius at the root of the ribs in the contact surface of the bonded rubber mounting in the gearshift housing is now 30mm (formerly 5mm).
March 21, 1964	6223768	**Engine**: The oil strainer cover is now secured with cap nuts and copper washers instead of hexagon nuts and spring washers. The material for the gasket is improved.
April 30, 1964	6317836	**Electrical**: The clip securing the battery is now located on top of the band instead of to the side.
May 30, 1964	6412733	**Heating**: The warm air outlets on the heat exchangers are increased in diameter from 50mm to 60mm.

1964

Date	Chassis/Unit Numbers	Modification
June 24, 1964	6465663	**Chassis**: The clutch cable guide tube is rerouted in the frame tunnel.
June 30, 1964	6476782	**Steering**: The steering gear housing is filled with transmission grease.
August 3, 1964	115000001	**Chassis**: The beginning of the 1965 model year. Chassis numbers are altered to the nine-number system.
August 3, 1964	115000001	**Rear Axle**: The bearing cover and bake plate now has a drain hole.
August 3, 1964	115000001	**Interior**: The threaded bushings for the seatbelt mountings are now 7/16-inch.
August 3, 1964	115000001	**Body**: All window area is increased.
August 3, 1964	115000001	**Electrical**: The windshield wiper blades are spring loaded and move to the left instead of to the right.
August 3, 1964	115000001	**Body:** The engine lid latch, formerly a handle, is now a press button lock. The jack now has a separate lever socket to raise and lower the car. The window regulators are activated by a cable system instead of a single arm regulator.
August 3, 1964	115000001	**Interior**: The backseat rest can be folded down for more cargo space. The front seat backrests are thinner and more flexible, and the outer tubes of the backrest are attached to the spring core. The sun visors are larger and, instead of being mounted on the rearview mirror bracket, are attached to the roof cross member.
August 3, 1964	115000001	**Electrical**: The main wiring harness is positioned on the left lower side member instead of the left roof member.
August 3, 1964	115000001	**Rear Axle**: The needle bearing for the gears are arranged in pairs.
August 3, 1964	115000001	**Brakes**: Type II brake hoses now used on Type Is. The diameter of the master cylinder decreases from 19.05mm to 17.62mm, and the stroke increases from 30mm to 33mm. The angle of stop on the foot pedal is increased from 7 degrees to 9 degrees and 30 minutes. There are now additional contact surfaces (three points) for the brake back plate and brake shoes. The slots in the wheel cylinder pistons are wider, and the ends of the shoes are angled. The drilling for the rear brake drum oil deflector is discontinued.
August 3, 1964	115000001	**Heating**: The heating operation is changed so that two levers (instead of a knob), located on either side of the hand brake, operate all of the heating. The red lever on the right controls the incoming heat while the white lever on the left controls the heater vents in the rear.
August 3, 1964	115000001	**Chassis**: There is now a star stamped on the frame tunnel at the beginning and end of the chassis number.
August 14, 1964	115040085	**Engine:** The clearance of the number one main bearing of the crankshaft is increased by 0.006mm. Before, the bearing journal was 0.005mm smaller in diameter.
September 8, 1964	115083659	**Fuel:** The fuel lines for the Export Sedan are now equipped with a diaphragm valve.
September 10, 1964	115116205	**Brakes:** The rear lining for the brakes is changed from Energit 717 to Energit 335.

1964

Date	Chassis/Unit Numbers	Modification
September 14, 1964	115084567	**Heating**: The heat exchangers are ribbed internally.
September 24, 1964	115145488	**Engine**: The oil intake pipe is now secured to the crankcase by a small bracket which is spot welded to the screening bell.
September 25, 1964	115148174	**Interior**: The guides for the steel sunroof are now plastic.
October 1, 1964	115161388	**Body**: Adhesive tape is applied to the back of the outside rearview mirrors.
October 8, 1964	115162787	**Engine**: The splines in the hubs of the 180mm and 200mm clutch plates are phosphate treated, while the splines of the main driveshaft are treated with a molybdenum disulphide-based coating.
October 21, 1964	115224816	**Frame**: The adjustment nut for the clutch cable is now a wing nut instead of a hexagon nut.
October 29, 1964	115243991	**Rear Axle**: The inside diameter of the rubber bush of the spring plate is decreased from 46.5mm to 44.5mm.
October 30, 1964	115241529	**Transmission**: The 1200A Sedan now features a fully synchronized transmission.
November 6, 1964	115262699	**Engine**: A dark blue enameled muffler is installed at random.
November 12, 1964	115255751	**Engine**: The outer oil drilling of the valve adjustment screw of the rocker arm is welded closed on the Export Model.
November 13, 1964	115366664	**Engine**: Instead of solid rivets, the 180mm clutch plate lining is secured with hollow rivets.
November 17, 1964	115286532	**Fuel**: The lower recess in the fuel tank (in the tie rods region) is enlarged.
November 20, 1964	115306919	**Brakes**: The front brake shoe retaining pin is now 40mm long instead of 35mm.
December 1, 1964	115479289	**Fuel**: The gasket for the fuel tank is now made of rubber instead of cork.
December 1, 1964	115331161	**Electrical**: The Champion L87Y spark plug is added to those still used: Bosch W175T1, Beru 175/14 and Champion L85.
December 2, 1964	115331768	**Transmission**: The retaining plate for the transmission is reinforced.
December 7, 1964	115336420	**Engine**: The oil bath air filter is now equipped with a crankcase ventilation tube.
December 16, 1964	115349565	**Electrical**: The windshield wiper arm uses a tension spring instead of a compression spring.
December 30, 1964	115509682	**Interior**: Inside the door trim panel pocket is made of PVC foil.

1964

This rear quarter view shows the larger window surface area on all sides of the Beetle.

The windshield wipers now rest on the left side instead of the right side, and the window itself is slightly curved, allowing it to extend 28mm into the roof line.

In 1964, the rear window is increased 20mm higher and 10mm wider.

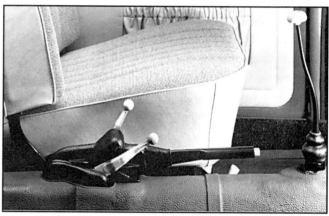

In place of the faucet-like knob that controlled the heat are these two levers. The gray knob (left side) controls the rear heel board heating and the red knob controls the heat amount.

The sun visors now swivel to the side, as it was discovered that the sun doesn't always stay in the same place all the time while a person is driving.

The rear seat folds down and is held by a strap to keep it from bouncing during the car's operation

1965

Model Year Chassis Numbers: 115000001 to 115999200 (to December 1965: 116463103)
Model Year 1200cc Engine Numbers: 3972441 to 3546988 (to December 1965: DO 050314)
Model Year 1300cc Engine Numbers: 8796623 to 9725086 (to December 1965: FO 442242)
1965 Model Year produced between August 3, 1964, and August 1, 1965

1965 marked the introduction of the VW 1300, a new series powered by a 40bhp engine, using the crankshaft from the Type III 1500 engine. As a result, the stroke was increased from 64 to 69mm. To distinguish these from their less-powered brothers, all VW 1300s have a "VW 1300" chrome badge on their deck lids. All Beetles were fitted with newly designed brake drums, and a new front axle was fitted from a VW 1500, linking the steering knuckles and control arms via the ball joints. A much more comfortable suspension comes from reversed shocks, modified torsion bars and hollow rubber buffers.

Some added perks for the 1300 are locks on the front seats to prevent them from folding forward, an added register in the middle of the dashboard to help in window defrosting, the return of the semicircle horn ring, and the addition of the headlight dimmer switch on the turn indicator arm.

Date	Chassis/Unit Numbers	Modification
January 4, 1965	115358743	**Brakes:** The master cylinder operating rod increases in diameter from 8mm to 9mm.
January 4, 1965	115363043	**Front Axle:** The cutaway in the lower shock absorber eye is now larger, allowing more flexibility of the protective tube.
January 18, 1965	115450398	**Body:** The plastic guide plugs on the trim molding for the door and windows is discontinued.
January 19, 1965	115375697	**Rear Axle:** The seal for the driveshaft is made with a black polyacryl rubber instead of blue- and brown-colored rubber.
February 1, 1965	115400026	**Brakes:** The retaining pin for the rear brakes is now 32mm long instead of 28mm.
February 1, 1965	115400109	**Brakes:** With the addition of the hand brake cable equalizer, the and brake cable is lengthened.
February 2, 1965	115400026	**Interior:** The rubber boot for the hand brake lever is now made of PVC.
February 18, 1965	115553822	**Engine:** All engines are marked with a letter that corresponds to the DIN horsepower. 30hp: A; 34hp: D; 42hp: G; 45hp: K; 52hp: N; 54hp: R.
March 1, 1965	115579323	**Clutch:** The lining for the 180mm clutch now has a radial groove on the flywheel side.
March 22, 1965	115648983	**Transmission:** There are now deeper guides for final drive cover, and the selector shaft for first and second gears are supported in two places.
April 5, 1965	115685587	**Transmission:** The eye on the left final drive cover is relocated and the paper seal is replaced by a rubber one.
April 6, 1965	115685587	**Clutch:** The bent, hex nut for clutch cable adjustment is replaced by a straight, wing nut.
June 15, 1965	115928504	**Body:** The folding support for the front hood is replaced by a spring for the 1200A model.
June 20, 1965	115946462	**Fuel:** The filler cap seal is made of rubber instead of cork.
August 2, 1965	116000001	**Front Axle:** The spacing between the axle tubes is increased

1965

Date	Chassis/Unit Numbers	Modification
		from 120mm to 150mm.
August 2, 1965	116000001	**Engine**: There are now 18 fins on the cylinders of the 1200 model instead of 12.
August 2, 1965	116000001	**Interior**: The front seat backs are fitted with a locking device to keep the seat from folding forward.
August 2, 1965	116000001	**Heater**: There is now an additional heating vent in the instrument panel.
August 2, 1965	116000001	**Fuel**: The carburetor is now a type 30 PICT-1, with a new jet arrangement. The cut off valve is in the upper part of the fuel pump with the filter to the side instead of the valve in the fuel pipe of the 1300 model
August 2, 1965	116000001	**Front Axle**: The steering knuckle is connected to the torsion arms with maintenance-free ball joints. There is now a clamping nut with socket head bolt to adjust the wheel bearing instead of a hex nut. The steering stop is limited by means of adjustable screws welded onto the front axle beam. The front wheel suspension uses ball joints instead of king pins and link pins. The number of torsion bar spring leaves is increased from 8 leaves to 10.
August 2, 1965	116000001	**Frame**: The front frame head is modified to receive the new suspension and front axle.
August 2, 1965	116000001	**Electrical**: The dimmer switch is moved from the floor to the turn signal lever. Emergency flasher system introduced on some Export Models. The push-button connection is exchanged for a flat cable connector consisting of three right-angle push-on terminals. The horn ring returns with a modified thumb button control.
August 2, 1965	116000001	**Brakes**: Stiffening ribs have been added to the rear hubs, and the distance between the disc contact surface and the drum hub contact surface has been increased 22mm. The rear track increased from 1288mm to 1300mm.
August 2, 1965	116000001	**Transmission**: The diameter of the ball pin of the gearshift lever is increased from 9.15mm to 10.5mm.
August 2, 1965	116000001	**Wheels**: The wheel discs are now slotted.
August 12, 1965	116000001	**Frame**: The clutch cable guide is protected by a 60mm rubber hose.
August 30, 1965	116095979	**Heater**: The diameter of the hole for the shaft of the heater control flat is 7.5mm, increased from 6.5mm.
September 14, 1965	116176209	**Fuel**: The depression in the bottom part of fuel tank near the left tie rods is enlarged. The sender unit is modified accordingly.
November 19, 1965	116364282	**Engine**: The upper three crankcase studs are now 166mm long and anchored 10mm deeper in the case.
December 1, 1965	116382728	**Body**: The cable to lock the hood is now galvanized.
December 15, 1965	116407142	**Engine**: The clutch release bearing's plastic ring is now treated with molybdenum disulphide.
December 21, 1965	116417035	**Tools**: The shape of the hubcap puller is altered.

1965

As well as the crank, the Beetle inherited the flattened hubcaps of the Type III and the air vents in the rims.

As so displayed by the badge on the deck lid, the 1965 year produced a new engine, the 1300, by adding the crankshaft of the Type III engine to increase the stroke from 64 to 69mm.

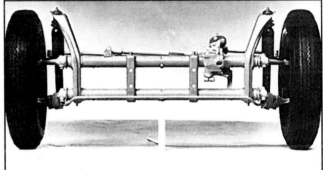

The redesigned front axle has a 10-leaf torsion bar system with maintenance-free ball joints that connect the steering knuckles to the torsion arms. As well, the four lubrication nipples in the axle tubes only need attention roughly ever 6000 miles.

The 1300 engine with its internal modifications still looks the same as the previous power plant (including the fresh air pipes from the air filter).

1965

For the 1300 Model and the Convertible, a vent is added to the center of the dashboard. The headlight flasher is moved from the floor to the steering column's turn signal lever and the semicircle horn ring returns slightly changed.

Door panels and quarter window panels now have bright chrome work.

The 1200A enjoys the new front axle from the 1300, slotted steel wheels, and adjustable front seats. The only difference is the lower horsepower engine and some of the older style trim.

The Convertible now gets the flat hub caps and the slotted rims. This example sports chrome wheel rings.

Among the 22 improvements for the 1965 Beetle was a rear seat that folded down almost completely flat, allowing for more luggage space.

The foot-activated dimmer switch remains only on the 1200 Sedan.

1966

Produced between January 1, 1966 and December 31, 1966
Chassis Numbers: 116463103 to 117422503
Engine: 1200 D 0016999 to 120750
Engine: 1300 F 0115030 to F 1057754
Engine: 1500 H 0000000 to 576613
1966 Model Year: Produced between August 1, 1965 and July 31, 1966
Chassis Numbers: 116 000000 to 116 1021298
Engine: 1200 D 0120751 to 095049
Engine: 1300 F 0955582 to 940716 (until July)

The Beetles made in 1966 underwent some surprising changes. The deck lid was redesigned to allow for the 1500 engine which was added this year also. In accordance with the wishes of various exporting countries, the license plate mount became more vertical, the lower section was shorter and the overall space inside the engine compartment was enlarged. The new 1500cc engine was tuned to 44bhp at 4000rpm, with torque at 102nm at 2000rpm. Top speed was 125km/h. Besides increased power and speed, the major change was in intake air preheating: Heated air is drawn through two pipes underneath the carburetor and mixed with the intake air. The Beetles all had a wider rear track, almost 1350mm, and the rear axle was fitted with equalizer springs to help with the action of the torsion bars. Disc brakes were added to the front wheels.

One customer complaint was the use of two keys, one for the ignition and one for the doors. In 1966, one key was used instead, operating both the doors and the ignition. In addition, the doors could be locked from the inside by a push button near the rear corner of the window frame. The driver's door also had an armrest that could be used to shut the door. Outside, narrower chrome trim was used for a more subtle look.

All knobs were made of a soft black plastic to prevent reflection from the sun into the front window, and the seats could be folded forward by using a knob to unlock the safety latch.

By this time, Volkswagen had produced 12 million Volkswagens, with two million exported to America.

Date	Chassis/Unit Numbers	Modification
January 3, 1966	116463104	**Engine**: The threaded plate for the oil sump is no longer welded in. Instead it is tapped.
January 3, 1966	116463104	**Brakes**: The front brake lining is made of Textar TE-18 instead of Textar V-643.
January 3, 1966	116463104	**Engine**: The welded two-piece heat exchanger tube is now a single piece. The pressure spring for the carburetor linkage is replaced by a return-type spring. The carburetor is modified accordingly and renamed 28 PICT-2. The intake manifold vertical tube is offset on the left side.
January 7, 1966	116478507	**Engine**: The connecting rods are fitted with bolts and nuts instead of bearing caps and hex bolts.
January 16, 1966	116480078	**Steering**: The steering ball joint is retained with a plastic ring from the Type III.
January 18, 1966	116488425	**Transmission**: The gearshift lever stop is fitted with two lips instead of one.
January 21, 1966	116525573	**Body**: The door locks are now lubricated with Mobiplex 47 instead of universal grease.

1966

Date	Chassis/Unit Numbers	Modification
February 1, 1966	116534113	**Tools**: Replacing the 14mm box wrench is a 13mm unit.
February 25, 1966	116680470	**Body**: The seal between the sliding sunroof and the roof is an elastic rubber seal.
March 1, 1966	116622321	**Engine**: The protruding flanges for attaching the oil cooler on the left crankcase half have been reinforced.
March 1, 1966	116809564	**Body**: The door handle shape is modified and covered with Nirosta steel.
March 3, 1966	116628529	**Engine**: The distributor driveshaft teeth have been uniformly lengthened.
March 7, 1966	116629921	**Steering**: To compensate for additional camber, the steering damper has a long tube.
April 1, 1966	116723046	**Fuel**: A rubber collar is fitted on the fuel pump instead of a two-piece plastic collar.
April 26, 1966	116741602	**Engine**: The seal between the crankshaft and the flywheel is now made of rubber instead of metal (metal seals are still used in vehicles with Saxomat).
May 2, 1966	116809564	**Electrical**: The diameter of the rubber grommet on the headlight housing is increased from 10mm to 13mm.
May 3, 1966	116807190	**Engine**: Hot air is now taken through the heat exchanger instead of from underneath the cylinder heads.
May 3, 1966	116851572	**Interior**: The pedal cluster is fabricated from metal strips instead of cast iron.
May 6, 1966	116861446	**Engine**: The flywheel gland nut has been increased by 1.5 threads (or approximately 2mm).
May 11, 1966	116866804	**Steering**: The interior diameter of the retaining ring of the steering ball joint is increased 3mm.
May 12, 1966	116872032	**Brakes**: The fluid reservoir now has a sediment trap and screw cap.
June 6, 1966	116976635	**Transmission**: There is now a countersink in the differential for the reception of a self-locking ring gear securing bolts.
June 3, 1966	116962505	**Body**: Anchors for lap belts are added on the inside of the quarter panels.
June 23, 1966	116975949	**Engine:** The pushrods are 0.8mm longer and their diameter increased from 8.14mm to 9mm.
August 1, 1966	117000001	**Rear Axle**: The suspension is now fitted with an equalizer spring.
August 1, 1966	117000001	**Hub Cap**s: The wheel covers are modified.
August 1, 1966	117000001	**Electrical**: The starter has a smaller diameter pinion. The generator house is 104mm in diameter. The turn signal switch is modified because of the two-spoke steering wheel. The six-volt electrical system is changed to 12 volts, and the front turn signals are combined with the parking lights. Instead of eight fuses, the fuse box now holds 10. The ignition coil now has three connectors on terminal 15 instead of two. A second backup light is mounted to the rear bumper.
August 1, 1966	117000001	**Brakes**: The drum brakes hose bracket on the lower part of the frame head is repositioned and the hose altered. The rear brake backing plate has two adjusting holes and two inspection holes.

1966

Date	Chassis/Unit Numbers	Modification
August 1, 1966	117000001	**Body:** The fenders are modified to house the headlights vertically. The door lock striker plate is attached using four screws instead of three screws. The trim molding has a narrower profile and uses smaller holes for the now plastic clips. The engine compartment is altered. The apron is shortened and the hood is adapted to house license plate vertically. Soundproofing is increased around the rear window. One key is used for both locks and the interior operation is modified. The rear quarter panel's shape is reinforced because of the installation of an equalizer spring.
August 1, 1966	117000001	**Chassis:** There is now a water drain hole with a rubber valve in front of the frame fork. The brake hose bracket on the frame head is positioned 86mm toward the outside of the car and 20mm to the rear.
August 1, 1966	117000003	**Engine:** The labyrinth in the crankcase breather is enlarged. The 1500cc engine is introduced for the 1967 model year. The flywheel now has 130 teeth instead of 109. The outside diameter is increased and the starter and transmission case are both alternated.
August 1, 1966	117000003	**Brakes:** The front brakes are converted from drum to disc and the steering is altered to fit.
August 1, 1966	117000003	**Interior:** The three-spoked steering wheel is replaced by the two-spoked variety (with a recessed hub).
August 1, 1966	117006301	**Front Axle:** The ball joints are now greased with a special corrosion prevention lubricant designated TL VW 735.
August 2, 1966	117018982	**Engine:** The crankcase studs (M12 x 1.5) are sealed with self-locking sealing nuts. Washers are discontinued and the tightening torques are now 2.5mkg.
August 15, 1966	117054916	**Engine:** The oil pressure relief valve is now activated by a piston and an annular groove.
August 25, 1966	117101112	**Chassis:** The shift lever ball is reinforced below the ball housing.
September 1, 1966	117112318	**Transmission:** Discontinued is the spraying of lubricant on the main driveshaft splines.
September 15, 1966	117180343	**Brakes:** The stop plate for the brake and clutch pedals is increased from 10mm to 11mm.
September 20, 1966	117183619	**Engine:** The seal for the gland nut and flywheel is now soaked in engine oil before application.
September 29, 1966	117239925	**Chassis:** The clutch pedal is realigned so there is approximately 25mm between clutch pedal and brake pedal.
September 29, 1966	117197986	**Engine:** The self-locking nuts on the crankcase studs are replaced by a sealing ring between the case halves.
October 10, 1966	11722137	**Heating:** The seals on the rear heating vents are modified.
October 25, 1966	117272280	**Fuel:** The fuel hoses are attached to the carburetor via hose clips.
November 17, 1966	117349409	**Brakes:** The fluid reservoir for a single-circuit brake system is repositioned 17mm higher.
November 21, 1966	117349001	**Heating:** The warm air hoses between the engine and the body

1966

Date	Chassis/Unit Numbers	Modification

are additionally fitted with hose clips.

November 25, 1966   117359672   **Engine**: The oil pipe is now a seamless piece instead of welded.

December 1, 1966   117425908   **Body**: The control of the front seat backrest lock is near the top of the backrest instead of in the frame.

December 14, 1966   —/—   **Brakes**: For the Export Models, a dual circuit system is used.

December 15, 1966   117384751   **Brakes**: The pushrod for the master cylinder of the dual circuit brake system is adjustable.

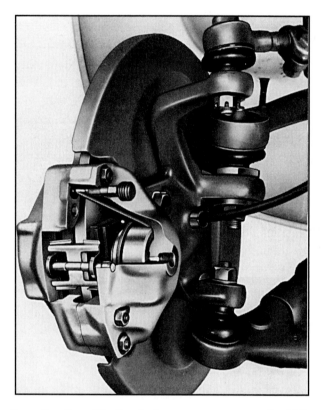

From the Type III, disc brakes now appear on the VW 1500's front wheels, which secure the rims with four bolts instead of five. This change won't come to American Exports until the following year.

The door is now opened with a rounded thumb-button and can be locked/unlocked with the ignition key. One key now operates the entire car.

1966

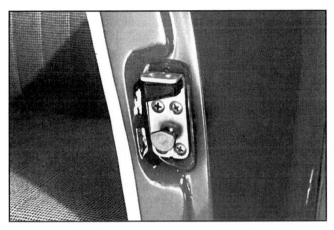

The striker plate in the door jam and matching locking mechanism on the door are redesigned to further prevent opening during severe body flex.

Doors can now be locked via a button at the rear corner of the window sill. The armrest on the driver's side is now slotted to be used to close the door.

A rear equalizer spring is added to the rear axle, as shown in this production drawing.

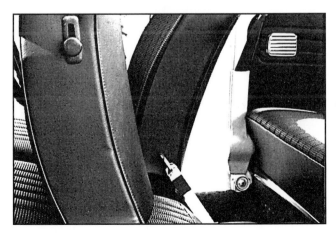

For late-model 1967 Beetles, the backrest catch is designed into the seat back. Early 1967s are still operated from the base of the backrest.

All switches are now flat and made of a soft plastic. They are colored black to prevent reflections and hot spots in the driver's eyes. The ashtray is opened without a pull knob.

1966

In the 1966 production year, the popular VW 1500 debuts with a larger engine and more horsepower.

The preheating on the 1500cc engine is now via four pipes, as the air filter is equipped with a weighted regulator flap on each side to control the intake of preheated air to the carburetor.

Narrower chrome trim is a dead giveaway that this is a 1967 Export Beetle.

The engine deck lid is shorter, the license plate is angled more vertically and the plate light is redesigned wider. "VW 1500" is the name plate.

1967

Produced between January 1, 1967 and December 31, 1967
Chassis Numbers: 117422504 to 118431603
Engine: 1200 D 0120751 to 0297008
Engine: 1300 F 1057755 to 1296298
Engine: 1500 H 0576613 to 0915221
1967 Model Year: Produced between August 1, 1966 and July 31, 1967
Chassis Numbers: 1170000001 to 117844902
Engine: 1200 D 0095050 to 0234014
Engine: 1300 E 0006001 to 0014000 (U.S. smog)
Engine: 1300 F 0940717 to 1237506
Engine: 1500 L 0000001 to 0019335 (U.S. smog)
Engine: 1500 H 0204001 to 0874199

The engine lid (which now had louvers for fresh air) and front hood were shortened. The bumpers were strengthened and raised slightly and the front fenders were modified to allow vertical positioning of the headlights (finally for the domestic market, as the export markets received these changes the prior year). The horn grills were discontinued. The door latches were opened by a trigger-type button, preventing accidental lock-out. The larger mirror could swivel freely when/if knocked by accident, and the filler neck was accessible from an outside door. Inside, all Beetles had safety steering wheels that collapsed when involved in a collision, and there were three-point mounting points for seat belts. The speedometer, gas gauge and turn signal warning lights were all incorporated into one gauge, and on impact, the rearview mirror disengaged itself from its bolting point.

The brake systems on the 1300 and the 1500 now used dual circuitry. They both had a 12-volt electrical system and were equipped with a new, sophisticated double-jointed rear axle, the IRS (independent rear suspension). The taillights were made bigger, and the reverse lights were fitted in the taillight housing.

In August 1967, production of the 34bhp 1200 model was halted, but could be ordered by request. The 1300A, as it was called, had the 34bhp engine installed on the 1300 model chassis. Then, less than six months later, in January 1967, the 1200, then called the Sparkafer (Economy Beetle) was returned to the market and remained so until the end of the Beetle's production.

Date	Chassis/Unit Numbers	Modification
January 9, 1967	117470115	**Body:** The trunk handle is made of aluminum when Nirosta was formerly used.
January 18, 1967	117496034	**Body:** The door hinges have an oil reservoir.
January 24, 1967	117489408	**Engine:** The diameter of the thrust shoulder on the third bearing is increased from 34mm to 36.2mm.
February 24, 1967	117560696	**Engine:** There is now a double oil drilling in an X formation instead of a single passage.
March 22, 1967	117614174	**Engine:** The inlet and outlet pipes of the heat exchangers are shortened and a supplementary collar has been added to the outlet pipe.
April 11, 1967	117632001	**Front Axle:** The wheel bearing cap is fitted with an opening for the speedometer drive spindle and sealed with red metal cement.
April 20, 1967	117666265	**Brakes:** The pushrod for the brake master cylinder is adjustable on the single-circuit brake systems. The depression of the clutch pedal is limited by a stop behind the petal on left-hand drive cars only.

1967

Date	Chassis/Unit Numbers	Modification
May 31, 1967	117738627	**Engine**: The throttle valve in the upper part of the carburetor has a thicker spindle and two shims.
June 29, 1967	117816884	**Fuel**: The fuel hose clip is fitted with one tensioning lug nut instead of two.
July 3, 1967	117839015	**Clutch**: The production of the Saxomat clutch is discontinued.
August 1, 1967	118000001	**Fuel**: The tank is accessible via a fuel door flap on the right-hand side of the front side panel instead of underneath the trunk lid.
August 1, 1967	118000001	**Interior**: The gear lever is moved further back, shortened and straightened.
August 1, 1967	118000001	**Body**: The introduction of the crank-operated sunroof is made. Formerly there was the folding sunroof. Three-point safety belts are standard. The armrest on the door panel is horizontal. The bumpers are reinforced and attached at a higher point. The engine cover and trunk are shortened. Vertically mounted headlights are introduced on all models (before, it was introduced on the Export Model only). The backrests on the front seats locked on both sides and could be released with a switch on the left-hand side of the backrest. The dashboard is now padded as an optional item. The outside mirrors are fastened on the doors and are now larger. The door latch is to be locked only with a key from the outside (Germany only)
August 1, 1967	118000001	**Transmission**: The Volkswagen Beetle 1500 can be now fitted with an auto-stick transmission.
August 1, 1967	118000001	**Electrical**: The control knobs are flatter in shape, formed from soft plastic and have pictures and symbols on them. The windshield reservoir is fitted inside the trunk behind the spare tire. The taillights are enlarged, and the reverse lights are fitted as an optional extra. The thermoelectric fuel gauge is built into the speedometer. The steering column holds the ignition switch. The interior light bulb is spring loaded. The electrical system is now converted to 12 volt instead of 6 volt.
August 1, 1967	118000001	**Steering**: The steering column is now fitted with a collapsible lattice section to protect the driver during an front impact.
August 1, 1967	118000001	**Brakes:** The brake fluid reservoir is moved to the front luggage compartment. The shoes on the rear brake drums are increased from 30mm to 40mm, and the rear brake cylinder is 17.46mm in diameter.
August 1, 1967	118000002	**Exhaust**: The tailpipes are now 249mm long instead of 276mm long.
August 1, 1967	118000003	**Engine**: The 1500cc and 1600cc engines are fitted with a 30 PICT-2 carburetor with enlarged float chambers.
October 10, 1967	118227175	**Wheels**: The wheel is now a pressed steel modified in shape and known as the hump rim.
October 10, 1967	118195200	**Engine**: The 1500cc is fitted with emission control equipment.
October 13, 1967	118233162	**Heating**: The intake air preheating is regulated by a thermostat.

1967

Date	Chassis/Unit Numbers	Modification

The Bowden cable is 800mm long.

October 27, 1967   118265979   **Electrical**: The speedometer driveshaft cable is secured with a circlip instead of a pin.

November 10, 1967   118327724   **Electrical:** The oil pressure switch is mounted horizontally. From August 1967 to November 1967, it was mounted vertically.

The rear light cluster had a larger lens surface and an option reverse light.

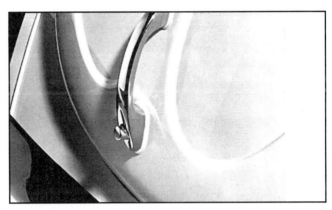

In addition to having to release the hood from inside the car, an additional button latch was incorporated on the hood handle.

Instead of having to lift the hood to fill the tank, a fuel fill neck was added to the exterior front quarter panel, including a flap. The neck again switched sides, from the left to the right.

For the 1300 and the 1500, fresh air louvers were added to the cowling above the front trunk hood.

HANDBOOKS
Auto Electrical Handbook: 0-89586-238-7/HP1238
Auto Upholstery & Interiors: 1-55788-265-7/HP1265
Car Builder's Handbook: 1-55788-278-9/HP1278
The Lowrider's Handbook: 1-55788-383-1/HP1383
Powerglide Transmission Handbook:1-55788-355-6/HP1355
Street Rodder's Handbook, Rev.: 1-55788-409-9/HP1409
Torqueflite A-727 Transmission Handbook: 1-55788-399-8/HP1399
Turbo Hydramatic 350 Handbook: 0-89586-051-1/HP1051
Welder's Handbook: 1-55788-264-9/HP1264

BODYWORK & PAINTING
Automotive Detailing: 1-55788-288-6/HP1288
Automotive Paint Handbook: 1-55788-291-6/HP1291
Fiberglass & Composite Materials: 1-55788-239-8/HP1239
Metal Fabricator's Handbook: 0-89586-870-9/HP1870
Paint & Body Handbook: 1-55788-082-4/HP1082
Pro Paint & Body: 1-55788-394-7/HP1394
Sheet Metal Handbook: 0-89586-757-5/HP1757

INDUCTION
Bosch Fuel Injection Systems: 1-55788-365-3/HP1365
Holley 4150: 0-89586-047-3/HP1047
Holley Carbs, Manifolds & F.I.: 1-55788-052-2/HP1052
Rochester Carburetors: 0-89586-301-4/HP1301
Turbochargers: 0-89586-135-6/HP1135
Weber Carburetors: 0-89586-377-4/HP1377

PERFORMANCE
Baja Bugs & Buggies: 0-89586-186-0/HP1186
Big-Block Chevy Performance: 1-55788-216-9/HP1216
Big-Block Mopar Performance: 1-55788-302-5/HP1302
Bracket Racing: 1-55788-266-5/HP1266
Brake Systems: 1-55788-281-9/HP1281
Camaro Performance: 1-55788-057-3/HP1057
Chassis Engineering: 1-55788-055-7/HP1055
Chevy Trucks: 1-55788-340-8/HP1340
Ford Windsor Small-Block Performance: 1-55788-323-8/HP1323
4Wheel&Off-Road's Chassis & Suspension: 1-55788-406-4/HP1406
Honda/Acura Engine Performance: 1-55788-384-X/HP1384
High Performance Hardware: 1-55788-304-1/HP1304
How to Hot Rod Big-Block Chevys: 0-912656-04-2/HP104
How to Hot Rod Small-Block Chevys: 0-912656-06-9/HP106
How to Hot Rod Small-Block Mopar Engine Revised: 1-55788-405-6
How to Hot Rod VW Engines: 0-912656-03-4/HP103
How to Make Your Car Handle: 0-912656-46-8/HP146
John Lingenfelter: Modify Small-Block Chevy: 1-55788-238-X/HP1238

LS1/LS6 Small-Block Chevy Performance: 1-55788-407-2/HP1407
Mustang 5.0 Projects: 1-55788-275-4/HP1275
Mustang Performance (Engines): 1-55788-193-6/HP1193
Mustang Performance 2 (Chassis): 1-55788-202-9/HP1202
Mustang Perf. Chassis, Suspension, Driveline Tuning: 1-55788-387-4
Mustang Performance Engine Tuning: 1-55788-387-4/HP1387
1001 High Performance Tech Tips: 1-55788-199-5/HP1199
Performance Ignition Systems: 1-55788-306-8/HP1306
Small-Block Chevy Performance: 1-55788-253-3/HP1253
Small-Block Chevy Engine Buildups: 1-55788-400-5/HP1400
Stock Car Setup Secrets: 1-55788-401-3/HP1401
Tuning Accel/DFI 6.0 Programmable F.I.: 1-55788-413-7/HP1413

ENGINE REBUILDING
Engine Builder's Handbook: 1-55788-245-2/HP1245
How to Rebuild Small-Block Chevy LT-1/LT-4: 1-55788-393-9/HP1393
Rebuild Aircooled VW Engines: 0-89586-225-5/HP1225
Rebuild Big-Block Chevy Engines: 0-89586-175-5/HP1175
Rebuild Big-Block Ford Engines: 0-89586-070-8/HP1070
Rebuild Big-Block Mopar Engines: 1-55788-190-1/HP1190
Rebuild Ford V-8 Engines: 0-89586-036-8/HP1036
Rebuild GenV/Gen VI Big-Block Chevy: 1-55788-357-2/HP1357
Rebuild Small-Block Chevy Engines: 1-55788-029-8/HP1029
Rebuild Small-Block Ford Engines: 0-912656-89-1/HP189
Rebuild Small-Block Mopar Engines: 0-89586-128-3/HP1128

RESTORATION, MAINTENANCE, REPAIR
Camaro Owner's Handbook ('67–'81): 1-55788-301-7/HP1301
Camaro Restoration Handbook ('67–'81): 0-89586-375-8/HP1375
Classic Car Restorer's Handbook: 1-55788-194-4/HP1194
How to Maintain & Repair Your Jeep: 1-55788-371-8/HP1371
Mustang Restoration Handbook ('64 1/2–'70): 0-89586-402-9/HP1402
Tri-Five Chevy Owner's Handbook ('55–'57): 1-55788-285-1/HP1285

GENERAL REFERENCE
Auto Math Handbook: 1-55788-020-4 /HP1020
Corvette Tech Q&A: 1-55788-376-9/HP1376
Ford Total Performance, 1962–1970: 1-55788-327-0/HP1327
Guide to GM Muscle Cars: 1-55788-003-4/HP1003
The VW Beetle: 1-55788-421-8/HP1421

MARINE
Big-Block Chevy Marine Performance: 1-55788-297-5/HP1297
Small-Block Chevy Marine Performance: 1-55788-317-3/HP1317

ORDER YOUR COPY TODAY!
All books can be purchased at your favorite retail or online bookstore (use ISBN number), or auto parts store (Use HP part number). You can also order direct from HPBooks by calling toll-free at 800-788-6262, ext. 1.

170